I was recently asked how long it took me to write this book. I had to think about it because it took all my experiences over the past 40+ years to finally propel me to write it. I started to write in August 2021, and it just flowed out onto the pages over the next three months with encouragement and guidance from Lindsay Bednar, CEO at Rodney K Press. With gratitude, Lindsay.

I'd like to dedicate the book to all the numerous investment professionals from many firms with whom I have crossed paths. Together we all learned and adapted as the financial industry continues to evolve and change for the better over the years and decades.

I especially want to thank the families with whom I have been working for the past 40 years and hopefully for many more years to come. Your trust and confidence in our process and advice validates our mission of saving multi-generational families one portfolio at a time.

I sincerely want to thank my family for the interruptions while I take client calls on weekends and while we are on vacation. In a sense our clients are an extended part of our family.

Finally, I want to thank my business partner, Nicole Wright, for her perspective, insights and ~~~ for our clients and their families. You have a g   d of you.

It is my sincere hope that you will enjoy t   use the information to find your personal Fina

Hal Tearse, CPWA®

Achieving
Financial
Freedom

The Tearse Wright Group

952 249-7629
newright@rwbaird.com

Robert W. Baird & Co. Incorporated
601 Carlson Parkway Suite 950
Minnetonka, MN 55305

www.tearsewrightgroup.com

Library of Congress Control Number: 2022908165

ISBN (paperback): 979-8-9852683-4-8

ISBN (ebook): 979-8-9852683-5-5

Achieving
Financial
Freedom
A Roadmap for all Investors

Hal Tearse
with **Nicole Wright**

A NOTE FROM THE AUTHOR

CONTENTS

DISCLAIMER

The content of this book is exclusively the views and opinions of the authors and are not necessarily the views of Robert W. Baird & Co. Incorporated. Any mention of stocks, mutual funds, and market information is for education purposes only and should not be considered a recommendation or solicitation to buy or sell any securities. Broad generalizations about asset allocations are also for illustrative purposes and do not constitute a recommendation, nor should be considered advice. Each investor has unique circumstances and needs and therefore would benefit from hiring the advisor of his/her choice in order to create a long-term wealth management plan.

INTRODUCTION

Knowledge is power.

Every day when I dropped my son off at school, I reminded him to ask good questions because that's how you learn.

I explained to him the more you learn, the better prepared you are to deal with problems and opportunities in your life. It takes a long time to learn complicated systems, jargon, and information that will be helpful in your quest for financial freedom.

The advice and stories that follow come from years of dealing with client investors, financial product wholesalers, and the Wall Street marketing machine.

I ask good questions and have forged a process of investing and creating wealth over the years that I believe has the best shot at helping investors achieve their goals and dreams.

There is no magic formula; no get-rich-quick schemes, no easy answers. The process is grounded in the idea that to get something of value in the future, you need to give up something of value today.

The first question that might come to your mind is, "Why do we need another book about investing and wealth management?"

The answer is two-fold.

For starters, this book is timely. Between 2018 and 2042, according to research and consulting firm Cerulli Associates, the baby boomer generation will pass down to their heirs an estimated **61 trillion dollars**.

Historically, it will be the largest generational transfer of wealth in the shortest amount of time. Unfortunately, without help from a top-qualified financial advisor team, the next generation is likely to get it wrong. This will undoubtedly hasten the drawdown on family wealth or even loss of it entirely, as has occurred in many families, including the Vanderbilt fortune.

Second, the millions of Americans who are woefully unprepared financially and emotionally for their retirement years need this book. Retirement is expensive and requires thoughtful planning to have freedom of choice when you retire.

Throughout this book, I will share the inside secrets and workings of the Wall Street marketing machine and shine a light on topics that will impact your financial future so you can make informed decisions around money and wealth.

Every family has a different story and history. Family wealth can come from a variety of sources, which impacts how each individual thinks about money and wealth management. These unique differences are important for the advisor team to understand in order to build out a personalized financial, tax, and estate plan.

As you build and preserve wealth, you will need planning and help from a team of professionals, starting with an experienced financial advisor. What could be more important to you and your family than providing the freedom of choice that wealth provides?

My passion for wealth management and planning ignited when I witnessed my family and friends fail at handling their wealth. I was determined to change that for myself, my children, and the families with whom we are privileged to work. Wealth can be a blessing or a curse, but the most significant benefit is that it provides the freedom to choose how you want to live your life. Hiring a qualified advisor can increase your odds of a successful outcome, regardless of your current income or wealth situation.

The financial markets and industry have become increasingly complex over the years, and the industry has done very little regarding financial literacy for investors. A survey of books, articles, and incessant internet posting does little to solve this problem. In most cases, the recommendations or advice are self-serving toward a narrow point of view or solution.

In the following chapters, I intend to provide you with important information so you understand **what types**

of questions you should be asking and who to ask. Both are critical to successful wealth management outcomes for families throughout the wealth accumulation and management journey.

> **We all have our own biases, and mine is to take an unconventional, common-sense approach to investment and wealth management solutions based on my experiences over the past four decades. Much of it is the result of a relentless journey of asking questions, watching the industry evolve, and using common sense to create understandable, elegant solutions that work in all market conditions. I do not follow the herd because the herd is usually wrong.**

The bibliography at the end of this book has several checklists and resources you might consider to help you through your personal journey toward financial freedom.

BACK TO THE BEGINNING

After graduating from the University of Minnesota in 1975, I worked as a fourth-generation member of our family grain business. I quickly realized that the grain industry was consolidating at a rapid pace, and our family business would not be around much longer. The company did not have any retirement plans available, and the long-term employees were left on their own for their retirement years once the business was forced to liquidate. Even my father ended up with very little after 35 years with the company.

At the same time, being an avid fan of soft drinks and consuming several servings a day since high school, I bought my first shares of stock in Coca-Cola. I was fascinated by the markets and thrilled when my certificate of ownership arrived for 100 shares. I was hooked on soft drinks and the stock market. I am still hooked on the markets; however, I quit drinking soda 20 years ago.

After a couple of years at the family business, I decided to accept a position at Merrill, Lynch, Pierce, Fenner, and Smith Brokerage firm (shortened to Merrill Lynch in later years, now Bank of America, Merrill Lynch). I eagerly headed to New York City for three months of training. That was the beginning of my career in the financial markets. As it turns out, training in the 1970s mainly consisted of learning what is required to pass the industry licensing requirements to begin working with clients. Today, firms do a better job training the advisors; they go beyond the licensing requirements regarding the firm's available investment options and planning tools. It is important to remember that, in any profession, the real learning comes from doing the job; the financial advisory is the same—experience matters.

Ongoing training and certifications have been a staple of my career and have enabled me to better serve my clients. I received numerous industry designations in wealth management and fiduciary standards and, most recently, the Certified Private Wealth Advisor® (CPWA®) designation, which, because of the depth of knowledge required, is held by only 3,300 advisors in the country. The curriculum focuses on the needs of high-net-worth (HNW) investors and the multitude of investment, tax, and estate planning issues they face. The designation has annual continuing education requirements that are necessary to stay abreast of the ever-changing legal, tax, and investment industries.

Achieving Financial Freedom is my way of sharing what I have learned over the past 40 years of working in the financial industry as an advisor, branch director, syndicate manager, mentor, leader, and project specialist. The investment and wealth management business has changed considerably over the years, but the goal of wealth accumulation remains the same.

The insights and knowledge in the chapters that follow will help you realize your goals. Proper planning and the wealth generation of the stock markets and bond markets will ensure that you have the best shot at reaching your goals.

In today's world of instant gratification and consumerism, choosing delayed gratification allows your investments to compound over time and allows for potentially tremendous wealth accumulation benefits.

Albert Einstein is reputed to have said:

"Compound interest is the eighth wonder of the world. He or she who understands it earns it. He or she who doesn't, pays it."

EVOLUTION OF THE FINANCIAL MARKETS

How did we get here in regards to wealth creation and accumulation? It has been a tough road for many families who did not recognize the changes taking place in the retirement funding system. The change from defined benefit plans to defined contribution plans shifted the responsibility for retirement funding from corporations to individual employees. These changes reduced corporate commitments to employees and left employees in the dark about how and why they need to step up and fund their own retirement years.

With the demise of corporate pension funds in the late '70s and '80s, working American families were left on their own to save for their retirement years. 401(k), 403(b) plans, and individual retirement accounts (IRA) were created with tax deferral benefits to encourage employees to set aside a percentage of their income for retirement. Many companies offer employees incentives to contribute by matching all or some percentage of their contributions. Unfortunately, most employees only contribute the minimum required to receive the company matching dollars. Additionally, the investment options are somewhat limited, and participant education about investing funds is minimal. In my experience with these types of plans, investor outcomes are less than they could be, which, over a working career, could potentially negatively impact fund balances and lifestyle choices at retirement.

The *average life expectancy* has increased steadily from 65 years old in 1950 to 79.5 years old in 2021, according to

"United Nations- World Population Prospects". In addition, an increasing number of Americans are living into their 90's or even past 100 years old. Considering most people retire by age 62, it is likely that one spouse in a married couple will survive 30 years past retirement, meaning the average person must live off their retirement savings and social security checks for a long time. Not a happy ending for way too many families.

According to Michelle Cottle of the New York Times Editorial Board, "In 2018, there were 52.4 million Americans aged 65 and older and 6.5 million 85 or older. By 2040, these numbers will hit 80 million and 14.4 million, respectively." She goes on to say, "Nearly half of US households headed by someone 55 or older have no retirement savings, according to 2016 data." This is shocking and completely avoidable.

Another phenomenon occurring is that the business owners of the baby boomer generation are selling their privately owned businesses, which encompass virtually all of their wealth. Family farms that have been in individual families for many generations are being sold for residential development or to pay estate taxes because, eventually, the IRS will get its share. Money is moving from hard assets to financial assets to the tune of trillions of dollars each year as the estimated 10,000 baby boomers are retiring every day.

This will affect everyone, including the following:

- The owner of a private business looking to create liquidity through a sale

- Family owner of real estate whose land will be more valuable as residential developments than continuing as farmland
- A millennial family looking to secure a financial future
- A pre-retirement-age family looking to ensure their retirement years will be comfortable and worry-free
- A multi-generational family looking for tax-efficient strategies to provide for future generations
- An entrepreneur that is experiencing new first-generation wealth
- A single, hard-working individual planning for his or her future

THERE IS SOMETHING VALUABLE IN THIS BOOK FOR ALL OF YOU.

Wealth management, wealth accumulation, retirement income distribution, and proper estate and legacy planning are all unique and essential to create, grow, and retain family wealth. However, this is not easy, and this book is not intended to be a complete answer for all those situations.

The intent is to give you a 30,000-foot view of what has become a complicated and important part of all our lives. The complexity and nuances of each client's situation require a team of highly qualified professionals to help each family navigate investment, tax, and estate issues.

I'm confident that you will find this book valuable. Each chapter has a couple of pages to take some notes that you might want to refer to later.

WOMEN AND INVESTING

"Being financially literate is a powerful thing, especially for women."—Otegha Uwagba

Although this chapter is titled "Women and Investing," that doesn't mean you should skip it if you are not a woman. You most likely have important women in your life, whether it be your partner, mother, daughter, or sister, and understanding how finances not only affect them but view them is important. Don't worry, as a man, I won't be telling you what women want—my business partner, Nicole Wright, is the author of this next section.

WHY AREN'T WOMEN TRADITIONALLY INVOLVED?

You might have noticed in the past few years that there are more financial advertisements geared toward women. All the big investment firms have shifted their focus to women. Why is that?

According to Mckinsey research, *"By 2030,*

> **American women are expected to control much of the $30 trillion in financial assets that the baby boomers will possess—a potential wealth transfer of such magnitude that it approaches the annual GDP of the United States."**

That is a pretty significant number, which would explain why marketing to women is no longer niche marketing—it has become a top priority.

When I see these focused ads targeting women, part of me wants to shout, "Finally! They see us!" But the other part of me knows that the industry as a whole is acknowledging that they have historically left women out of the equation. Now that women will control the majority of the assets, they suddenly have an interest in speaking to women. Unfortunately, it seems like it is more self-serving than for the sake of progress.

So why have women historically not been involved with finances? It goes back to when most people conformed to gender roles: men worked and took care of the finances, and women took care of the kids, the cooking, and the cleaning. Over time, responsibilities have shifted, although some of the stereotypical roles have remained.

Over the decades, women started to take roles outside the home, whether they were working because they wanted to or out of necessity with the increasing cost of living. Whatever the reason might be, women joined the workforce and made up nearly 60% of the workforce in 2019, according to www.biz.gov.

Working women also carry most of the load when it comes to the children and taking care of the house. There is also the mental load that women carry because we are more likely to think about what our family needs and anticipate the next move we need to make. Between careers and home lives, who has time to worry about finances?

If you are single, you absolutely have to pay attention to your finances because there isn't anyone else to do it for you. However, even if you are married or have a partner, both parties need to know what is going on. My favorite example is that my husband mows our lawn; he prefers to do it, and he isn't too keen on the way I do it (which is fine with me!). This is part of his responsibilities for the house and family.

But what if something happens to him where he is unable to physically push the mower or he is no longer here? We certainly hope that doesn't happen, but we are prepared. I know where the mower is, I can recall the combination to the shed (most of the time), and I can operate the mower. I even know who I need to call for a tune-up. I know how to do these things because if I was left alone it would be an even tougher situation if I felt like I was drowning in responsibilities of which I have no knowledge.

Understanding your finances is much more important than mowing the lawn because, let's be honest, you could probably hire someone fairly quickly to take care of it for you. That isn't the case when it comes to understanding your finances. Yes, you should have a financial advisor that you trust will assist you, but that will only take you so far. You are the one that has to budget and understand what bills need to be paid, and if you are left to this in the wake of a tragedy, it can be more overwhelming than you can imagine.

One of our clients was a married couple who was the classic love story type couple, and they truly took care of each other. They both worked, but he took care of the finances. Unfortunately, the husband got sick, and it wasn't too long before he passed away. His wife was distraught, as anyone would be, but then she had to take on the burden of figuring out bills and investment accounts. It broke my heart to see her go through that, and I want to help other women so they don't have to go through additional suffering during an already painful time.

SELF-CARE

I hear about self-care a lot, especially on social media. It is one of those concepts that, as a woman, I know I need to do, but the execution gets a little fuzzy. I always have grand ideas at the beginning of the week:

I am going to a yoga class.

I am going to read for fun, not just for work.

I am going to prepare healthy meals every day this week.

Then I get to the end of the week and realize I have put everything else at the forefront and never got to my "self-care" list.

I consider taking part in your finances as self-care because it is part of taking care of yourself. It might not feel as rewarding as a massage or going out with friends, but it is just as important, if not more.

Think of it as the 100-meter dash—everyone is lined up

together. But when the race begins, women have to wait an additional five seconds to begin the race. What contributes to those five seconds?

According to The Pew Research Center, the gender pay gap has remained steady for the past 15 years. While the younger generation has started to make headway, the older generations have remained the same. In 2020, women made 84% of what men made, meaning that women would have to work an additional 42 days to make the same amount as men.

In addition, women are more likely to have employment gaps—taking years off to take care of young children—losing income and retirement savings as well as having to start at the bottom when re-entering the workforce, making it harder for women to move up the ladder in their careers.

The results of employment gaps and the gender pay gap: we have less money to save for retirement and we typically don't think about saving for ourselves because we feel like we need to direct those funds to our families. We as women tend to put others before ourselves. We are pulled in so many directions—arguably more than our counterparts—that if we don't have an accountability partner, we can fall through the cracks.

WHY YOU SHOULD CARE

At the beginning of this chapter, I mentioned that the financial services industry has recognized the transfer of assets into the hands of women. Part of that is that women have taken control, but the other part is due to the death of a spouse or divorce. According to the US Census Bureau, women's life expectancy is projected to reach 87.3 years by 2060 compared to 83.9 years for men.

Divorce is another difficult topic to discuss. No one plans to get divorced, but you need to be prepared in case that becomes your reality, no matter how unlikely it may seem. In 2020, according to cdc.gov, the current divorce rate was 2.7 per 1,000. The 50-years-and-older age group has a slightly higher divorce rate. Knowing where you are financially can help you if you end up in a harmful situation, and it will help you find the strength you need to keep you and your kids safe.

If you have children, you already know that the best way to teach kids is to lead by example. If you don't understand your finances, how do you expect your teenager to be engaged with their own financial future? Unfortunately, our schools do not provide this important information to students, which is a failure of our educational system. Currently, only ten states require that high school students take one semester of personal finance in order to graduate, according to Next Gen Personal Finance.

We allow students to take out enormous amounts of debt in student loans, and there is little to no comprehension of what that really means. Everyone wants to put a bandage on the student loan crisis, but we should stop it at the root of the problem. The root of the problem is the lack of awareness of what it means to take on that kind of debt. For example, if your child wants to be a teacher, going to a private college where they will have $100,000 in student loans after they graduate is not the ideal choice. Your child could receive the same education at a university or state school for a fraction of the cost. As parents, we have to help our kids by providing guidance and setting boundaries so they don't start their adult lives saddled with student loans they struggle to pay.

WOMEN VS. MEN

No, this is not a discussion on who is better than who (but let's be honest, you know the answer!). One of the main differences between women and men when it comes to finances is that we think about it differently.

Obviously, this is not the case for every single woman and every single man. We are all unique. But think about it, when you see an ad, can you tell whether it is targeting men or women? Would you play different music if you were hosting an event with all women compared to an event with all men?

I will give you a hint: the answer is YES! We think about the world differently, and it is a beautiful thing. If we all had the same perspective, then it would be a dull and predictable world.

Men tend to approach finances from a data perspective—numbers, charts, and graphs. There is less emotion in the process, and the interest is in hard facts.

What is the bottom line?

How can I get a better return? Women are more likely to take a softer view and a more emotional approach to finances.

Do we have enough money to take care of our kids?

What if we have to take care of our parents?

I want to leave a legacy for the kids.

How can we use our money to help make the world a better place?

This view is much more emotional and less about the charts and graphs. Women are more philanthropic; after taking care of their families, they want their money to do good in the world.

So we have two very different approaches to finance with no right answer. Understanding why your partner views money is important because it will make financial decisions easier. I have had situations where we are meeting with clients, and once we bring out the charts, the eyes of the wife glaze over while her partner is engaged intently. When we go over the planning part of the meeting—where we discuss goals and where the money is going—we find that the women are more engaged. You can throw out numbers all day long, but in the end,

We just want to know if we are going to be okay.

Not everyone has a partner to work with, and not everyone fits into the generalizations I mention above. The critical takeaway is that it is important to think about how you approach finances:

- Is it working for you?
- Are you working with a trusted advisor that understands your financial language?

- If you have an emotional view, are you bombarded with charts and data that you couldn't care less about?

CALL TO ACTION

The point of this chapter is not to call women out or to say that men are bad for not letting us get involved from the beginning. Money is an uncomfortable subject for most, and it is almost never discussed with friends and extended family. When we avoid talking about it, our kids learn to not talk about it, and the vicious cycle continues. I have also found that people (both men and women) are often afraid of the answer, so they put off asking questions because ignorance is bliss, at least temporarily.

If you are single, you need to make sure you don't put wealth management off. No one is going to be there to take care of you, so take charge. If you have a spouse or partner and you currently have a financial advisor, you need to be involved. Annual meetings? Show up and be engaged for that one hour a year. Your future depends on it. Your kids depend on it. You depend on it.

As women, we have made tremendous strides in this country when it comes to equality, and compared to much of the world, it is one of the safest places for women. We need to take a seat at the table, not because it was offered to us, but because we are strong enough to take it.

SECTION 1:
THE FIVE STAGES OF WEALTH ACCUMULATION AND MANAGEMENT

1. Discovery Phase
2. Accumulation Phase
3. Retirement Income Phase
4. Diminishing Capacity Phase
5. Wealth Transfer Phase

It is important to consider all five of these stages and how they connect. In the more mainstream planning literature and discussion, there are only three phases. In our practice, we have witnessed and worked with clients that had to deal with Phase Four—Diminishing capacity. Based on our experiences, we have decided to add it to the conversation because, with extended life expectancies, it is a conversation to be had before the need arrives.

Each phase leads to the next and requires different approaches and client behaviors to successfully navigate.

DISCOVERY PHASE

The first step of the planning process is the **Discovery Phase**. This is an exchange of information that digs deep into what matters most to you and your family. Having this conversation with your financial advisor sets the stage for subsequent decisions that drive the plan. We use several tools to help facilitate this conversation, which helps us get to know you and your family.

We all rely on several professionals during our lives. When we are sick, we rely on medical professionals to help us heal and recover. But the truth is, we are all going to die, and there is only so much a doctor can do.

However, I would like to suggest that as financial advisors, we help all of our clients leave a multi-generational legacy that includes their family values around wealth, education, and philanthropy if that is what they desire.

So, what does this involve? It is not hard, but it takes an investment of time on your part on the front end.

PLANNING CHECKLIST

- Gather copies of statements from all your financial accounts and investments.
- Spend some time understanding your lifestyle expenses and your ongoing contributions to retirement plans and savings accounts. If you are already retired, then plan for the future years and beyond.
- Work with your financial advisor to explore your goals. Your wealth can and should be about achieving these goals.
- Your advisor should be able to put this information into a plan and provide feedback regarding the probability of success. Monte Carlo simulations are popular and informative for the advisor and client. Monte Carlo calculates a thousand possible outcomes based on the current facts and provides a range of probability of success. Of course, this will change over time as the client circumstances and markets ebb and flow. The Monte Carlo is only one of the tools you and your advisor may use to assess the current state of your investment portfolio as it pertains to your future goals.
- Create a visual picture of your journey. This is where conversations about choices are made.

- Talk your choices through with your advisor so everyone is on the same page.
- Use a planning tool. Clients and their advisors can do "what if" scenarios, but more importantly, choices are made and priorities determined.
- Review your updated plan at least once a year with your advisor, confirm that the inputs are still valid, make changes as necessary, and reset. You should be able to track your progress toward the stated goals.

This all sounds easy, right? If that were the case, why do so few people do this? I believe that most families do not prioritize the long term, and frankly, many of the advisors I have worked with over the years do not want to invest the time required to build and update the plans.

In the "fee for advice" world that most financial advisors work in, the regulators require that advisors do an annual review with every client. Advisors with over 200 households are then faced with doing a client review nearly every business day of the year. To accomplish this, advisors will often create a multi-page investment performance report and present it to clients to meet the requirements. But that is just one part of the equation.

Be sure your advisor reviews and updates your plan at least annually or more often as needed. If this is not occurring, look for an advisor with fewer clients who will take the time to share your journey year after year.

Recently a friend of ours shared that she disliked her

advisor and had not talked to him in a couple of years. Unfortunately, this is common. Advisors should have no more than 100 households to take care of and do complete reviews each year. Advisor teams should also have 100 households or fewer per advisor and staff to support each advisor.

In our practice, we commit to our clients to learn more about them than any of the other tax and real estate planning advisors with whom they work. In this way, we can anticipate their needs and be a resource and liaison with their other professional advisors.

For those who recall, in the TV series from the 1980s called *The A-Team* with George Peppard, starring Colonel John "Hannibal" Smith, Hannibal was fond of saying at the end of the show, "I love it when a plan comes together." It always made me laugh because they never really had a plan, but things seemed to work out in the end as they continually adjusted to the changing action. That was TV, not real life. Having a plan is better than not having a plan and relying on luck.

LUCK IS NOT A PLAN.

Questions page—make notes

- Do you have a will(s), and has it been updated in the last five years?
- Do you need/have revocable living trusts?
- Do you have durable powers of attorney in place?
- Does each spouse have bank and credit cards in their own name?

- Have you retitled assets, including your estate, to ensure they are in your trusts?
- Do you have a comprehensive financial plan?
- Do you have a tax advisor?
- If you have all of these completed, does your financial advisor have copies?

If you answered no to any of these questions, now is the time to get organized.

ACCUMULATION PHASE

This phase is critical for setting the base for the other phases of wealth management. The goal of the Accumulation Phase is to create sufficient assets to provide you with a sustainable and growing source of income over the last 30 years or more of your life. Owning the right assets during both the Accumulation and Retirement Income Phase is critical for your plan to work.

It is also important to have a vision of how you want to spend your retirement years. Do you want to travel to see the world, focus on golf and leisure, spend time with family and friends, or relocate to a different state? Whatever your vision is, it is important to write it down to make it real.

A page at the end of this chapter is a good place to make notes.

In contrast to the typical advice of allocating as much

as 40% of your investments to fixed income, I suggest that less than 10% be held in cash reserves. The remainder should be invested in some of the best companies in the world for investors with long time horizons. These allocations differ based on the age of the clients, time horizons, current market conditions, and total assets available.

The reason to avoid low-yield investments is simple. They do not return enough to keep up with inflation and the price increases of goods and services. Your investments need to grow in value and income faster than the rate of inflation. Currently, we are suddenly experiencing much higher inflation because of excessive money in the system due to the pandemic funding by the government and a desire to inflate the economy. As long as interest rates are lower than inflation, savers in money markets and other liquid accounts are experiencing a negative rate of return after accounting for inflation.

Inflation over time erodes your purchasing power, which is defined as the number of goods and services you can buy with one unit of currency.

It now takes $2.03 to buy something that $1 would have gotten you 20 years ago. In 2021, the price of a gallon of gasoline has increased by 50%, and prices for many foods have increased significantly. In other words, the cost of living has increased. This is called inflation.

Since 2008, inflation and interest rates have been stubbornly low. Going forward, it appears that increasing inflation rates will continue to erode the purchasing power of your money.

I am sure you would prefer to place your money where it will increase in value over time in excess to inflation as opposed to investments that are designed to return a slight premium or even less than the rate of inflation. This is how to build wealth. Let's get started.

Utilize all pre-tax retirement plans available to you.

For all employed individuals, whether they are business owners or employees, the most important accumulation vehicles available are pre-tax plans such as 401(k), IRA, SEP IRAs, deferred compensation plans, NSOs, ISOs, and after-tax Roth IRA/401(k)*. Whatever your company offers, take advantage of the plans to begin building your personal wealth. For senior-level corporate executives, qualified and nonqualified stock options are also important wealth accumulation vehicles, each with specific tax considerations. Some companies also have nonqualified deferred compensation plans that are unique to the company.

Most of these plans are pre-tax contributions. Therefore, your taxable income each pay period is reduced by the amount you contribute to the plans.

Example #1: For every dollar that you contribute, you save on taxes to the extent of your combined federal and state tax liability. For simplicity, when you contribute $1,000 to the plan and you are in the combined state and federal tax bracket of 50% you have saved $500 in taxes in that year.

Example #2: If your combined tax bracket is 30 percent and you contribute $1,000, your tax savings would be $300

---

*   See glossary

that year. If you contribute the maximum of $19,500, your tax savings would be $5,850 for the year.

In 2021, the maximum employee contribution was $19,500 with an additional $5,000 catch-up contribution for those turning 50 or older. Employer contributions are also added to your accounts. They will vary from plan to plan. The limitations tend to increase periodically as Congress deems appropriate.

For maximum benefit, contributions to pre-tax savings plans should begin early in your career. Do not be tempted to borrow or take money out of these plans. People who are young and single should try to put as much as they can up to the government limitations in their early years. Once you start a family and take on additional expenses, having saved properly will prevent you from having to make difficult decisions about the allocation of available resources later in life.

In a perfect world, you could max out your retirement savings, afford private college tuition, and own expensive homes and toys. But we do not live in a perfect world, and there are times in our lives when we need to prioritize how we spend and save money. Choices need to be made for the present and future years.

Even if you cannot make the maximum contributions in your early years, getting the plan started with even a couple of thousand dollars a year is important. The great equalizer of time and the magic of compounding interest will allow those dollars to grow until your retirement years.

Many employers have a sponsored retirement plan with a payroll feature that allows pre-tax deductions to go automatically into your account. This is an effortless way to accumulate significant assets for your retirement.

For private business owners, it is best to confer with your CPA or tax accountant to determine if you should contribute to the pre-tax or Roth option if your company offers both. There are some issues around highly compensated individuals and the rest of the employees in regard to how much you can contribute pre-tax. Utilizing the Roth option could help with the safe harbor rules around the pre-tax option.

The Roth IRA/401(k) is one of the least understood but potentially most valuable accounts that you will have. Because Roth contributions are after-tax, they will not be subjected to the rules and taxation of pre-tax contributions. If you need to balance tax brackets in retirement, the Roth accounts provide tax-free income. If you do not need to access the funds in these accounts they will pass on to your beneficiaries tax-free under current laws.

To our clients who are still employed, we recommend that they utilize a mix of pre-tax and after-tax accounts to minimize income taxes on their retirement income and provide tax-efficient choices to fund their retirement years.

Solo business owners should also confer with their tax advisor regarding solo 401(k) plans or SEP IRA plans. These allow for significant pre-tax contributions.

UNDERSTANDING THE TIME VALUE OF MONEY

If you start at age 25 and invest $5,000 a year with an 8% average annual return for 43 years, taking you to age 68, you should have approximately $1.65 million. If you start ten years later and invest $5,000 a year with the same 8% average annual return after 33 years, again at age 68, the result is about $729,000. For the 35-year-old to achieve the same $1.65 million, the annual contribution would need to be about $11,200 a year. These numbers are simple math calculations. Average returns assume investing in stocks. Consider the impact if you contribute even more in your younger years, up to the current limits, and you also get matching money from your employer.

> **The key takeaway is that time and compounded growth are your biggest allies. Embrace them both as you look to your retirement years.**

- Tip 1: Maximize your contributions each year to a level at or beyond what you need to receive the matching dollars from your employer (free money!). If possible, max out each year. Every dollar you set aside into the retirement plans and leave until retirement can come back to you exponentially when you need it the most.

- Tip 2: Never, never, never borrow from your 401(k) plan. It is not an ATM.

- Tip 3: If you have access to a Roth in your company plan, split your contributions between the pre-tax and Roth accounts. Your financial planner can help with determining what the split should be.

- Tip 4: Start early in your working career. A modest monthly contribution invested in stocks beginning at age 25 will grow to over $1 million by age 65. Who wants to be a millionaire?

- Tip 5: Elect your contributions to go directly to the retirement accounts. If the money after taxes comes to your paycheck, you will likely spend it.

- Tip 6: Pay yourself first and everyone else second.

The Accumulation Phase is the ultimate delayed gratification phase. Save today to ensure a financially secure and worry-free retirement.

It is never too late to start saving. I made all the mistakes that you can avoid. Early in my career, our companies provided pensions. The catch was that the pension accounts had a ten-year cliff vesting schedule. If the participant left the company before his or her tenth anniversary, the company retained the accumulated balances.

As happens in business, I did not stay ten years and gave up the benefits. In the mid-'80s, companies started to offer employees the opportunity to self-fund their retirements through plans like the 401(k), 403(b), and Para plans. American employees suddenly became responsible for their own retirement funding with only a modest amount of help from their employer.

The key takeaway is that each of us is responsible for funding most of our retirement income, not our employers. Start now and keep at it.

Unfortunately, this idea was lost on an entire generation of workers. According to Investopedia, the 56–61-year-old on average has only $163,577 in retirement savings. Those aged 65 to 74 have even less. The medium numbers are 50% lower. Currently, only 32% of Americans invest in their company's 401(k) or similar plans. This is discouraging because 59% of employed Americans have access to a pre-tax retirement plan.

I did not get serious about my retirement funds until I was in my early 40's. Since then, I have maxed out every year. I also saved an additional 10% of my income in company deferred compensation plans, built up a strong reserve cash fund, and invested in some of the best companies in the world.

I am happy to report that what I have learned later in life will also work for you. If you start earlier, you may be able to retire earlier and enjoy life without work, or, at least, a life that isn't controlled by your work schedule.

A client asked us for a specific total value in his accounts that he needed to accumulate so he could get up every morning and go to work because he wanted to, not because he had to. We worked with him and his wife to determine their living expenses and what they envisioned for their retirement years. Then, we set a goal in terms of financial assets and time frame. They hit the goal in a few years, and he continued with the job he enjoyed for a couple more years. By then they had exceeded their financial goals by 30%.

From age 59 ½ until age 72, you may remove funds from your retirement accounts, and the funds become taxable at the ordinary income levels. Remember, the money went in pre-tax, (hopefully, many years earlier) and now comes out for your use at the current tax rate.

At age 72, required minimum distributions (RMD) kicks in, forcing you to take about 4% of the account balance and pay taxes on the money as income in the first year. Each year after, the percentage required to withdraw increases until the accounts are exhausted after 28 years. These rules are also subject to Congress and change periodically.

Withdrawals before age 59 ½ are subject to a 10% early withdrawal penalty and taxed as ordinary income. Therefore, it is best to wait until after the age of 59 ½.

The exception to the examples above is if the dollars you direct toward the Roth component in your 401(k) if offered are after-tax contributions. Those funds will grow tax-free and will not be subject to RMD at age 72. They can be used at any time after age 59 ½ without tax consequences. A large Roth balance helps to minimize withdrawals from other pre-tax accounts beyond the RMD. The Roth becomes another option for the planner to use in the Distribution Phase.

Let's do the Math:

Start with the rule of 72. It tells us how many years at a particular rate of return it will take to double the value of your investment. For example, divide 72 by 6% return and you get 12 years. An 8% average annual return will double your money in nine years.

Let's take this one step further:

At age 25, start with a $5,000 annual pre-tax contribution compounding at an average annual rate of return of 8% and continue for 35 years until you are 60 years old. You will have invested $180,000, and the account will be worth about $1 million pre-tax!

What if you wait until you are 35 years old to start and invest $5,000 for 25 years? You would have invested $130,000 and your account would be worth about $429,000 pre-tax.

Now you understand the amazing power of compound interest over long periods of time and how you too can become the millionaire next door.

> **In order to turbo-charge this process, start by making annual contributions and qualify for your company match. Then, utilize the auto escalator built into the company plan if it is an option. You can increase your contribution by 1% a year until you maximize your investment contributions. Simply sign up for it and let it work for you.**

The hypothetical 8% average annual return is a good goal for your investment plan. Some years, the plan's performance will be much better than other years, where the performance may even be negative. In years when the markets are posting negative returns, keep investing and, if possible, increase your contributions to take advantage of the temporary lower prices. Shout for joy and invest when stocks are on sale because the sales generally do not last very long.

Are you getting the general picture of these plans and

why they are important for you and your family? The details above are the basics. The more you contribute, the more you will have available during your retirement years. Time is the great multiplier, and correct asset selection is the engine that makes the plan work.

About 15 years ago, I received an account from an older client of one of the other advisors at our company who had left. The client was in his mid-90's at the time. He had been a schoolteacher at a private school in the Twin Cities his entire career and, as we know, teachers work for very modest salaries, especially at private schools during the '50s, '60s, and '70s. Ironically, he had taught at the school my son and I had attended. The client had moved to Florida to live out his retirement years shortly after retiring from teaching. When I looked at the account initially, I was a little surprised that the value of his securities were a bit over $4 million. On closer look, he only held 20 stocks, and the holding periods on average were 25 years. The cost basis, meaning the amount of money that he had invested in these stocks over the years, was $161,000. He was not a miser by any means because he had also taken distributions from the account over the years of slightly over $1,000,000.

This is an example of the miracle of owning shares in some of the best companies in the world and holding them for a long time. The client passed away at age 99, leaving the shares in his account for his two children equally. And because of the step up in cost basis allowed under the tax laws of this country, there were no capital gains taxes applied to the transfer of the assets.

This simple strategy legally allows for a step up in cost basis on financial assets, real estate, and other hard assets. Congress threatens to eliminate the step up in basis; however, nothing has come of it yet. If it does, we will hopefully find other strategies to minimize the tax consequences of transferring the assets.

Having an experienced financial planner team in your corner will help you make decisions regarding your participation in the plans offered by your employer. They can assist with general asset allocation suggestions as they build your personal financial plan for your family. Your advisor will also help hold you accountable to stay the course and execute the plan.

RETIREMENT VISION

List all of the things you wish for in your retirement years.

1 _____

_____

_____

_____

2 _____

_____

_____

_____

3 _____

_____

_____

_____

4 _____

_____

_____

_____

RETIREMENT INCOME PHASE

The **Accumulation Phase** leads to the **Retirement Income Phase,** and the relatively easy part in the first phase gives way to more complex issues. When the monthly/ biweekly paychecks end, it is time to turn on the retirement income streams to fund your well-deserved retirement years.

Following the Accumulation Phase, planning for the Retirement Income Phase should start no later than your mid-50's or earlier so you can make some adjustments if necessary to meet your goals. The typical reaction to short-falls is that the client wants to take more risks because he or she feels they don't have enough time remaining. This is problematic because it can lead to even worse outcomes if the economy and markets experience a downturn at the wrong time for the investor. The proper approach is to go back to the plan and make spending and savings adjustments as needed. Refer to the section about risk and investing for a more in-depth view.

If you are a private business owner and planning an exit, having a great pre-exit plan will make the transition much easier. See the section devoted to **Liquidity Events: Exit Planning** and **Sudden Wealth**.

The elements of retirement income for HNW families often include cash flow from a variety of sources. They include social security, corporate pensions, 401(k)s or similar plans, Roth accounts, IRAs, after-tax savings, investment accounts, annuities, investment real estate, oil/gas royalty interests, inheritances, income from family trust accounts, and shares in family-owned businesses that pay annual dividends.

The challenging part is to determine the most tax-efficient method of accessing the necessary cash flow needed to fund your lifestyle.

You might wonder what the big deal is about tax efficiency. It is paramount to consider when planning for your financial future. Your plan needs to provide your family with an income for as long as 35 years. Think about that for a moment. You may have only worked for forty years. As we discuss in the chapter regarding the financial plan, there are many variables, not only at the beginning of retirement income but all along the way as the client ages. We used to plan for life expectancy in the early 80s. Now we plan for the early 90s for at least one spouse. Some individuals are running their plans out to age 102. We all know people living close to or even a bit longer than 100. Because of the many variables that we face as we age, it is important to be tax-efficient in the early years to preserve as much wealth as possible for the later years.

SOCIAL SECURITY

One of the first discussions we have with clients regarding their retirement income is about **Social Security**. Social Security payments are primarily based on the last five years of employment, and they will begin sometime between age 62 and 70 years old. Under Social Security guidelines, everyone has a full retirement date. It used to be 65, but now it is bracketed up based on birth year. Now the most common age to retire is 66 or 67 to receive the full retirement benefits. Of course, eligible participants can choose to take Social Security at age 62 on a discounted basis or defer taking the monthly checks past full retirement to the age of 72.

Each year that the recipient delays beyond his or her full retirement date and initial participation, the monthly benefit increases by about 8% until age 70. Currently, there is no increase in benefits from age 70 to 72 years old, so the logical step is to take the money at 69 or 70.

Despite the discussions regarding the solvency of the Social Security program, it is highly unlikely that it will collapse or somehow disappear. Congress will likely make adjustments in terms of contribution percentages. Perhaps they'll move to age 70 for the receipt of full benefits, implement means-testing for the distributions, or apply other methods to ensure that the program continues. In its current configuration, you can think of it as an annuity based on your contributions throughout your working life if you paid into the system.

Some clients are surprised that their Social Security benefits are taxed. Annual Social Security payments of $25,000 to $34,000 incur income tax on 50% of the benefits and over $34,000, which affects nearly all high net worth families, up to 85% of the Social Security payments might be taxed. Note the phrase 'may be' is used because other considerations could impact this tax item. A CPA or tax professional is a great resource to help determine the actual percent that is taxable and at what tax rate.

An important consideration is:

> **When do you take the social security money? Should you take a discounted amount early or wait?**

The answer to that question depends on a variety of factors. Our planning process will determine the optimal time to start the payments for each client. We consider other revenue streams, the tax implications of each, and current average mortality data regarding longevity prospects for each client.

Simple, right? Not so much, and this is just the beginning.

Other factors, such as spousal benefits, former spouse benefits, and file and delay strategies play a role in making this decision.

Once you elect to receive your benefits, you cannot change them. Think and plan carefully.

MEDICARE

Another important piece that comes into play is Medicare, the government health insurance program for people age 65 and older. You are first eligible to sign up three months before you turn 65. You may be eligible to get Medicare earlier if you have a disability, end-stage renal disease or ALS (also called Lou Gehrig's Disease).

Health insurance is a central consideration when retiring before being eligible for Medicare because of the high costs associated with obtaining healthcare coverage in the private marketplace. The costs are high because you need to cover 100% of the premiums instead of sharing the expense with your employer.

It is important to note that Medicare has several parts. Initially, you get Part A, which is free and covers inpatient care in hospitals, skilled nursing facility care, hospice care, and home health care.

Part B covers expanded services; however, it comes at a monthly cost.

Part C covers additional extra coverage by private companies for vision, hearing, dental, and health wellness programs. There is a monthly cost for these items through private plans. Sometimes C and D are available from one provider.

Part D helps to cover the cost of prescription drugs (including shots and vaccines). You can enroll in this plan or choose coverage through private plans.

Medigap is additional coverage that is purchased

through private insurance and will help pay for expenses not covered in part A, B, C, and D.

For many families, the decision on when to retire can hinge on the cost associated with obtaining private medical insurance.

Families who plan to retire before age 65 will have to purchase private health insurance until they are eligible for Medicare coverage. Some people choose to remain employed past age 65 and continue with private insurance offered by their company and others elect to be on Medicare as soon as they are eligible. This is something to consider for each situation.

We work all of these financial considerations into the plan for our clients to help them decide the most advantageous time to retire.

This piece of the retirement plan is an expense and needs to be factored into the overall plan. In our practice, we rely on outside Medicare experts and internal experts to help advise our clients through this complicated and important element of their plan.

READY, SET, RETIRE

For families that have reached their financial goals early and plan to retire before age 59 ½, we need to do a deep dive to ensure that we do not create unnecessary penalties or taxes. We can use several strategies, including one called 72(t). It essentially means taking substantial and equal annual distributions each year from retirement plans until you reach the age of 59 ½. This will avoid the 10% penalty on early withdrawals; however, the distributions are taxable as ordinary income.

When we are building the retirement plan, we will look at all the other sources of income to minimize tax obligations. As stated above, corporate pre-tax retirement programs will create taxable income as the money is distributed as needed or through RMDs at age 72.

Our first look is at after-tax accounts. This includes savings, income real estate, taxable stock accounts, and bond investment accounts.

A few years before retirement, we typically position assets that would generate income and growth. In the current interest-rate environment, having the right investment portfolios has made a big difference for our long-term outcomes and generating income for our clients in their retirement years. There is much more on this in the investment chapter. However, this is a really important step, and it needs to be done before retirement to create the maximum benefit for the client.

One of the things that we stress to our clients is that their plans need to be transparent and flexible so that we can help them adjust and plan for the unexpected. As clients move into the Retirement Phase, which could last 30 years or longer, the plans will need to be reviewed each year. If necessary, adjustments will be made on the investment side as well as the expense side. As we have experienced in the last few years, we live in a world of great opportunity, but it comes with uncertainty and volatility.

No matter the initial retirement income strategy, things

will likely change as clients move into retirement, whether it is from fluctuating market performance, client behavior, or other unforeseen life changes.

One of my favorite stories is about a family that I worked with in the late 80s until the early 2000s. Paul had just retired as the manager of a large retail location of a national company, and he wanted some help planning his retirement income. His wife Pat had been a homemaker her entire life.

We used a straightforward planning process in those days, so we designed a simple investment plan that would provide them adequate income in addition to their Social Security and one pension.

Paul retired, sold their house in Minnesota, and built a house in Florida where they planned to live for the rest of their lives. We spent plenty of time making sure they had all their bases covered regarding retirement income, estate planning, and tax planning.

In September of 1999, I called Paul to schedule a trip to visit them, review their investments, and make sure we were still on track with their goals. I told him when I wanted to come visit, which was two weeks out from our conversation. Paul said he wasn't feeling very well and suggested I wait a few weeks and then we would chat again to schedule the visit. Unfortunately, Paul passed away a week after that conversation.

Paul and Pat had three children, one of which was a successful entrepreneur who ran his own company. Several weeks after the funeral, the son called me with a few questions he had about his father's investments. Of course, I was happy

*to chat with him. He started the conversation
with, "My father invested $750,000 with you
when he retired ten years ago, but when I look at
the statements, it appears he only has $700,000
remaining. Considering the time frame that the
investments were in place, I'm wondering what
happened? He should have significantly more
assets in his accounts."*

*My reply was that he was correct in that there
was $700,000 remaining in the accounts; however,
his father had taken income from the accounts of
$1.4 million over the ten-year period.*

*There was a pause in the conversation, and he
responded, "Well, that's pretty good."*

*Indeed, it was pretty good. Paul and I had
worked closely over the years to make sure that
they had sufficient income to meet their needs
and that the original investments stayed intact.
Because the equity markets were strong during
those years, they were able to draw close to 10%
from their investments in some years and enjoy
their life a little more.*

*Following Paul's death, I worked closely with
the children and their mother to get the house
sold and the mother moved into a life-care facility.
The issue there was that she had to purchase her
unit and pay monthly dues. The cost of purchasing
the unit was prohibitive because it would take
up over half of her cash, and then she wouldn't
qualify under the facility requirements to ensure
she could pay her monthly dues.*

*Our solution was for the children to each loan
their mother 25% of the cost of the unit, which
equaled 75% of the purchase price. When their
mother passed away, the children would receive*

> **100% of the original purchase price. The mother
> was 81 years old when we did this transaction.
> The kicker is, she married another resident in
> the facility about two years after moving in, sold
> her unit, the children all got paid back, and she
> received her initial investment back.**

This is a great example of a collaborative relationship with clients to solve problems that come up in their lives so they can enjoy their last years and not be a burden on their children.

The lesson in this story is that working with an experienced and qualified wealth advisor with a well-thought-out financial plan and wealth strategy can help clients successfully navigate through some complicated situations toward the end of their lives and beyond.

In the story above, the passing of Paul at a relatively young age and the surprise new relationship a couple of years later for Pat were both unforeseen occurrences. I am sure each reader of this book can think of similar stories. As their family financial planners, we felt confident that we could ensure Pat and Paul a comfortable lifestyle in their retirement years. We were able to craft a strategy for Pat and their children that worked better than expected; a win for all concerned.

The Retirement Income Phase is scary for many couples, from affluent investors to HNW families. We get used to a lifestyle and want to continue it. During our annual review and update meetings with clients, we discuss not only the income flow but also how the family feels about retirement. A conversation with your financial advisor is necessary to determine how you are adjusting to the change in responsibilities and newfound freedom of time you did not have while working. For some, it takes a few years to adjust.

In a recent conversation with a client who was trying to decide if he should retire next year or the year after, we explored the long-term benefit of delay by a year compared to the value of having that year of freedom from work responsibilities. He told me that he has never been able to go on vacation and not worry about work or check his email. In other words, he has never been able to be fully present on vacation. Conversations like these help clients solidify their goals and help them move on to the next chapter in their lives.

The other unknown is how long any of us will live. From a fiduciary point of view, we plan for clients to live into their 90s, but only a small percent will achieve that goal. So, if the client who is 60 years old and delays retirement for a year or two to save more money only survives to 75 years old, he has traded two years of income to get only 13 years of retirement. If he survives to 90 years old, then the two years is less of a trade-off financially.

However, we know that the last few years of life are typically challenging from a health perspective. The two years in good health on the front end seems to have more value than the extra wealth accumulated.

The problem is that we cannot predict how long any of us will live. That is why we have frequent and meaningful conversations with clients about what they value for themselves in their retirement years. We adjust their plans to reflect those values and wishes.

There's an old saying:

Life is what happens while you're making other plans. And that is certainly true in retirement years.

DIMINISHING CAPACITY PHASE

This is a topic that is typically not discussed. We have added it into our practice because it is important to plan for the possibility that this will occur to someone in their family. It is not uncommon to witness a client's ability to manage their affairs diminish as they age through their 80s and 90s. As advisors, it's hard to watch this happen.

From our experience, older clients go into denial and resist attempts to get help to do things as mundane as paying their real estate taxes, filing their income taxes, and the other day-to-day things.

This is an unfortunate stage to endure. The chances are it will occur in almost every family, especially as people continue to live longer.

The typical scenario is that if the couple is lucky enough to have adult children living close in proximity, the burden falls on them because their siblings live elsewhere. Thus, the term "the sandwich generation," referring to adult children caring for parents and their own children.

In many families with several children, the burden of caretaking typically falls on one or two of the children. This can create resentment on the part of the children and guilt on the part of the parents, depending on their cognitive impairment. Additionally, the children are busy raising their own children and are now faced with taking care of elderly parents.

I have witnessed personally in my own family and with clients that there's a great reluctance to have impaired parents cared for professionally. Naturally, the cost is an issue, but if there's enough wealth to cover the costs, it is likely a better alternative. Typically the spouse caretaker hangs on until they cannot physically or mentally continue to care for their loved one. Then the family must find professional care.

Many individuals with Alzheimer's or other forms of dementia try to stay home longer than they should. Unfortunately, these vulnerable adults are often taken advantage of by people close to them, especially as the older family member loses day-to-day memory function. This creates a lot of stress for everybody in the family.

Although these conversations are difficult to have, they are extremely important for our clients' quality of life in their retirement years.

If we plan early for this possibility, we can proactively recommend resources to help these families manage the day-to-day living expenses, care, and upkeep. There are companies that specialize in a concierge type of service, that can help with everything from paying monthly bills and doing the tax returns to assisting with downsizing a residence or purchasing a summer home. If there is enough wealth available, it is well spent to ensure older family members are well cared for.

Although potential beneficiaries of the wealth are sometimes reluctant to spend for services, in our experience, these services have managed to keep peace in the family before and after their loved ones have passed on.

One of the other big advantages of having a professional firm handle the financial affairs for families with declining mental capacity is that it eliminates the opportunity for fraud or elder financial abuse. Seniors are easy prey for organizations asking for donations to save XYZ animals or the children of the Amazon, the local church, theater, or college, or name your cause. We have even seen highly respected cultural organizations continue to ask for significant donations from older HNW clients who are not in a capacity to make those decisions. In a couple of cases, I have had to reach out to these organizations and explain that what they're doing could be considered elder financial abuse.

Unfortunately, these scenarios are not limited to scammers or even legitimate organizations soliciting financial donations. Just as often, elder financial abuse stems from one or more family members who take advantage of the opportunity for their benefit because they are the caregivers or simply because they can.

Having highly qualified financial advisors with years

of experience working with wealthy families and working in conjunction with a professional firm to manage the day-to-day affairs for older HNW families is the best protection for the clients and the future beneficiaries. When older individuals hold significant wealth, it is a good idea to have several individuals keeping an eye on the money and asking questions if something does not look right.

The National Council on Aging reports that 5 million elder Americans are victims of financial abuse, with an estimated annual loss of $36.5 billion. **Unfortunately this is a common occurrence.** If you suspect that a family member might be a victim of elder abuse, please search out help. Each state has passed laws regarding elder abuse.

> **TIP: When older relatives need assistance with finances, make sure there are checks and balances on the bank accounts and investment accounts. Transparency is critical.**
>
> **Change credit and debit cards every six months to prevent fraud. Mark Lanterman from Computer Forensics, a nationally recognized fraud expert, recommends avoiding debit cards altogether. They are too easy for strangers to copy at local businesses and start charging on your accounts. This is very common and avoidable.**
>
> **Engage with banks, credit card companies, and investment companies to make sure everything is current.**

TIP: In the process of helping a couple of older family members with their monthly bills, I discovered multiple organizations soliciting donations by mail. Naturally, the recipient feels compelled to send a check to "save the whales, seals, the children of Timbuktu, the oceans, and the planet." If you check out these organizations, you will find they have substantial foundations and your family member probably does not need to send them money.

To stop the solicitations, simply write "DECEASED" on the return form and they will likely stop mailing solicitations.

TIP: Be sure to lock/freeze your credit reports. They are held at www.Transunion.com, www.Experian.com, and www.Equifax.com. This ensures nobody can access your credit score. If you are applying for credit, you can unfreeze them for a few days and freeze them again. This prevents fraudsters from using your credit report to obtain credit cards and even purchase real estate. The freeze is free. When you do this, you can get a copy of your report to see who was accessing it. This applies to everyone.

WEALTH TRANSFER

The final phase is Wealth Transfer, also known as estate planning. An attorney who specializes in estate plans must be involved in this phase. Some attorneys attempt to practice law in a wide number of specialties. It is best to get the best attorney for the situation. We work with several attorneys in Minnesota to make sure the client gets what they need and nothing more. For clients who live in other states, we locate an estate planning specialist in their state that will meet the needs of our clients. We also participate in meetings to help answer questions that clients inevitably ask after the meetings.

Estate law is extremely complicated, and the documents need to be drafted in a way that reflects what the client wants for their family as the wealth passes to the next generation. This section is crucial for HNW clients with young children. The paperwork should be specific regarding the custody, care, and education of minor children. The documents should also specify how the assets are to be dispersed to their children or grandchildren based on several criteria as opposed to just turning over significant wealth to family members who may not be prepared to deal with sudden windfalls. The values of the parents and grandparents should be reflected in the documents and live on for years after they have passed away.

Some clients have provided for three generations and some prefer to leave a little to children and most of their wealth to charity and causes that are important to them. Each family is different, and we can better assist clients in their wishes by working with their other advisors.

> **TIP: Hire the best attorney suited to the situation. Hire an estate law specialist. A badly designed will and trust can be as bad as no will at all.**

> **TIP: Review and update your documents every five years. In the event of changes in your family, update your documents immediately.**

Clients typically don't think they need these plans in place until much later in life, but there have been so many times that the Super Wealthy failed to plan properly. A familiar case is the entertainer Prince who died in 2016. His estate was estimated by the trustees to be somewhere in the $163–$300 million range with royalties that continue to accrue. Because Prince did not have any estate planning documents, the State of Minnesota was left to sort out who received the assets. The reason it has taken so long is that multiple people claim to be directly related to Prince. Additionally, his brother, Alfred Jackson, passed away and a California man also filed a claim on the estate (and had a reputation for getting close to celebrities). Each person may end up with a sixth of the estate, complicating and delaying the settlement. Alfred Jackson had sold 90% of his stake in the fortune to Primary Wave, a music publishing and recording company. Prince's sister Tyka Nelson also sold a percent of her share to Primary Wave for cash upfront. And there are many more potential heirs that need to be sorted out and several lawsuits contesting the actions of the trustees. This wealth transfer will take many more years to settle.

Obviously, this is an extreme example, but the lessons apply to both HNW families and those with lesser wealth. At a minimum, there needs to be a legal will, health care directives, and power of attorney documents. The documents should be current and conform with the laws in the state or residence.

Families with greater wealth need more complex strategies to manage and protect their wealth for future generations. Too often we have seen families procrastinate the legacy planning process because they are uncomfortable thinking about and talking about death.

Families with children often understand the need for life insurance, which allows the family to continue forward in the event of an unexpected death. Life insurance is commonly available at group rates through employer plans, and this is a good start.

Next, the more important conversations need to occur to determine how much insurance is needed in the context of the overall family financial plan. As the children grow older and the financial risk of welfare, care, and education dissipate, the insurance piece should be adjusted accordingly.

Many years ago, a client kept putting off the estate planning process. The husband was agreeable to the planning, but his wife refused to discuss dying. One evening I mentioned to her that when they died their estate would go to their four beneficiaries.

She said, "Hal, you know we only have three children, not four."

I replied, "If you were to die without having an estate plan, there would be a fourth party to the assets. The IRS would join the party and could take as much as 55% in estate taxes leaving 45% for the three children."

That got her attention, and we had estate planning documents completed and in-hand three months later. The next step was to purchase second-to-die life insurance that would replace the estate tax liability at the second death. Since that time, the laws have changed considerably, and they have had their documents updated to reflect the current estate taxation laws.

I recently advised a young CEO of a privately held startup company in California that he needed to have an estate plan. In his early 30s, he was skeptical until I explained that his lifestyle, which included surfing, skiing, sailing, and other physical activities, could jeopardize his wealth if he became injured, incapacitated, or worse. Even though he is single and had not thought about estate planning, he understood what I was telling him. I referred him to an attorney to ensure that he had all his estate documents in place.

In addition to the estate documents regarding his shares in the company and other personal wealth, he completed a health care directive and durable power of attorney, giving his parents legal authority in the event of a catastrophic injury.

These documents are on the must-have list for our clients and should be on yours also. Be sure the language complies with your state requirements.

These are not fun topics to think about, much less act on. We explain to our clients that it is necessary to minimize estate taxes, maximize the asset transfer to the beneficiaries, and provide peace of mind to all the members of the family.

In our role as the primary family financial advisor, we do not practice law or give tax advice. We serve as the "quarterback" for the client and coordinate the efforts of the other professionals. Additionally, we have tax and estate professionals in our firm that can review and make suggestions that the client may want to consider. We do not charge any fees for these reviews.

A FINAL THOUGHT FOR THIS SECTION:

Even if you get the estate plan in place, it is important to ensure that the assets are either titled in the name of the trusts or have transfer-on-death instructions that move the assets to the correct trust on death. Any assets that are not in the trusts or have TOD designations will through probate court, which takes time and money. The goal is to avoid the expense and delay of probate court and ensure your wishes are honored.

FAILING TO PLAN
IS PLANNING TO FAIL

Think about your last vacation and the planning that went into the destination, travel arrangements, accommodations, and activities. Think about how much time it took to plan that one week.

If your family is like mine, family vacations are a give-and-take, with many negotiations to make sure everybody is happy. This is not always easy.

Now think about how much time you spend each year planning for your retirement years and the time when your wealth passes to the next generations, if that is part of your plan.

I would be willing to bet that the vacation wins.

In addition, when you drive somewhere new, you grab

your smartphone and open Google Maps to give you directions and chart the quickest route to your destination. As you drive, the app will alert you to turns, chastise you if you miss a turn, reroute you, and announce when you have arrived at your destination.

The difference between Google Maps or your family vacation and your financial plan is that in the first two examples, you were planning to arrive at a destination at a specific **time** and **place** in the near future.

Your financial planning is an ongoing process that is designed to get you to a **time** in your life rather than a **place** in your life. This is an important difference.

Most people are good at short-term planning but spend very little time on long-term planning. Working with a qualified and trusted financial advisor who will go along the journey with you is important. Think of your advisor as your coach and accountability resource.

Great advisors are good at the investing aspect of the relationship and great at managing client behaviors, which are critical to long-term success.

We all have dreams for the future—hopes for our children and grandchildren, our retirement years, and beyond. But few of us build the road map to get there. That's why working with an experienced financial advisor, tax expert, and estate expert is critical to help you prepare for that time in the future—the time when you transition from earning a paycheck to creating an income stream that hopefully you will never outlive, and perhaps leave a legacy for your children and grandchildren.

SECTION 2:
UNDERSTANDING THE GAME

LIQUIDITY EVENTS

EXIT PLANNING AND
FAMILY WEALTH TRANSFERS

There is a significant inter-generational transfer of wealth and reallocation of wealth occurring as assets like private companies and agricultural land sell for residential development, along with assets flowing to younger generations as parents pass the assets through their estate plans.

Entrepreneurs with emerging businesses in leading fields are also creating sudden significant wealth for the owners. Zoom is a great example. Early employees who worked for a salary and stock had hoped that the company would go public at $15 a share. I have a friend who was one of those employees. He worked hard for six years as the company grew. He continued to get awarded more and more shares. In July of 2019, the company went private at $35 a share, and it traded immediately at $100 a share.

Privately held businesses typically get sold to the younger generation in the family or to a financial buyer. The wealth in the company is then converted to cash that replaces the income streams that the business provided. In either case, it is critical to the process that the sellers plan for their financial lives after the sale. Once the money is transferred into their bank or brokerage accounts and taxes are paid, it is time to execute the wealth management plan that was created before the liquidity of the event.

In the case of a private business sale, it is not uncommon for the owner(s) to engage a professional business advisor team to help decide when, if, how, and to whom to sell the business. This phase can be a multi-year process. As the time gets closer to the sale of the company, working with an experienced wealth management planner and other tax and legal advisors can help the transition. In preparation for the exit, the sellers have peace of mind that they will be able to deploy the funds into an investment portfolio to support the next phases of their life. We have found in several cases that sellers fear the future after the sale. That tends to slow down the process until the sellers see a comprehensive wealth plan that details how and where they will get the income they need to meet their goals.

Real estate sales are a different type of liquidity event. The value of the land is completely dependent on the ability to convert the asset to another use that, in theory, would be more valuable than its current use. Farmland that is close to cities is frequently being converted to residential development by the current owners or sold outright to developers. The ability to subdivide the property is dependent on local community planning and zoning laws. Of course, these are all part of the process to develop the land and realize the locked-up value.

In both of these examples, owners typically focus on operating their businesses. In many cases, they do not have a financial advisor because all of their net worth and attention is tied up in the business or land.

Being a successful business owner or landowner is different from being an investor. Typically, business owners or landowners need a top-notch team of wealth managers in the mix before and after the liquidity event.

If the money hits the bank and the seller is not prepared to handle the wealth, the local bank will swoop in with solutions, and acquaintances in the financial field will swarm you. Being able to say "thank you but we have been engaged with a top wealth management group for some time, and we are all set" is a polite and sincere answer that will alleviate a lot of headaches.

Lottery winners tell stories of long-lost cousins or relatives that come out of the woodwork asking for money. Many top-paid athletes have also experienced negative outcomes because they did not understand how to protect and preserve wealth.

Another type of liquidity event is the inheritance of family financial assets, residential real estate, commercial real estate, or farmland that has been passed down through generations. At some point, it is possible to unlock the values and reposition the wealth to serve the current generation and the next if it makes sense. Proper estate planning that protects the assets for multiple generations while also benefiting the current generation is a common approach that we are often part of crafting.

Even the seller's financial assets and investment portfolios may need professional help to ensure the assets are correctly allocated to meet the needs of the new owners. There are tax considerations in regards to the current generation and how best to pass the assets along to the next generation as tax-efficiently as possible when the time comes. Here again, the team of advisors will come together to find the best solution for each family.

A great team of advisors can maximize your net after-tax proceeds from the sale of a business or family land. Below are some questions to think about:

- Do you have a plan to sell your business?
- Have you engaged a business exit professional to maximize your proceeds?
- Are you emotionally ready to sell your business?
- Do you have a post-exit plan to fill your time and interests after the sale closes?
- Do you have financial advisors as you liquidate agricultural land?
- If you are trying to develop the land, do you have the right advisors and expertise?
- Do you have a plan for the assets after the sale of the lots/development?

UNDERSTANDING MONEY AND WEALTH

Let's talk about money and wealth. Everybody has a different relationship with money, much of it dating back to how they grew up and how their family dealt with money. If your family had a scarcity of financial resources, you probably approach wealth very differently than if your family had an abundance of resources.

But what exactly is this stuff we call money? Why do we obsess over it? Why is it relatively easy to obtain, but so hard to keep? Do you remember when we wrote checks for everything and wrote it down in the check register? Or balanced our checking accounts? Naw. My father once told me he would cash a check for $10 on Friday each week, and it would last the weekend. Gas was 15 cents a gallon, and we rarely went to restaurants. We only had one car for a family of four. We had one black-and-white TV.

Then credit cards showed up, followed by debit cards. Now we can pay with a credit card that is actually on our phones. And we use the points to buy airline tickets, shows on Broadway, and all sorts of other cool things. We carry multiple cards to get a variety of benefits. We can use Venmo to pay for services or reimburse friends for splitting dinners. Who would ever have conceived this world back in the 1980s or before? Oh, I forgot about cryptocurrencies. The newest and most misunderstood, not to mention unregulated, methods of payments. And how about cash? I used to carry a couple of hundred dollars in cash to remind me of how fast it went through my fingers. Now it costs $90 just to fill up an 18-gallon gas tank.

In other words, money is not a thing. It is a system of accounting of an accepted currency to barter for goods and services.

> "Money is a commodity accepted by general consent as a medium of economic exchange. It is the medium in which prices and values are expressed. It circulates from person to person and country to country, facilitating trade, and it is the principal measure of wealth." (Britannica)

There are other thoughts and definitions about money and wealth. I have learned over my life that no matter how much wealth an individual has, somebody has more. That's just a fact of life. The relentless pursuit of accumulating an excessive amount of financial assets beyond what is needed to live a good life, provide for your family, retire, and leave a legacy can sometimes lead to bad decisions and even financial ruin.

We have been discussing wealth in terms of financial assets, but it is important to consider other types of wealth. Each family has a wealth of experience and history. As we live increasingly longer, it is important that intergenerational intellectual wealth and history is passed down to future generations.

Clearly, having money is better than not having money. However, your goal of accumulating financial assets during your lifetime should be to allow you to make choices about how you live your life in your retirement years and then how best to pass it along to the next generations.

WEALTH PROVIDES YOU THE FREEDOM TO MAKE CHOICES IN HOW TO LIVE YOUR LIFE.

In a nutshell, this is what it is all about. But it does not happen by accident. Financial freedom occurs by making decisions every day about how to spend your available financial resources for the near term and save for the long term. Many families are shocked by how much of their money slips through their fingers each month. Doing a quarterly review of how you spend your money will reveal areas that you can exchange for things today in favor of things in the future.

We recently worked with a young family that insisted they could not max out their retirement plans. We had them do a 90-day review of expenses, and they were shocked. Making a few minor changes in how they spent money each day contributed to an additional $12,000 a year. They just needed to adjust their habits, for example, making coffee at home rather than buying it at a coffee shop each day for four dollars a cup. Their coffee expenses annually were $1200 a year. A few more adjustments and they have an additional $1,000 a month to save and invest.

> **Tip: Spend less than you earn. Save or invest the rest.**

LEARNED BEHAVIORS AROUND MONEY

Money is often a point of friction between married couples. Sometimes disagreements around money destroy relationships. This can be avoided by having thoughtful discussions around the topic of earning, saving, and spending money. Young people who are considering a serious long-term relationship should definitely have these discussions before they say "I do" because they may end up saying "I won't!"

For those of us in the baby boomer generation, the typical family was structured where the husband earned the money, invested the money, and decided how it was going to be spent. Over the past couple of decades, that has changed as more and more women entered the workforce and started contributing to the family income. Women now have access to retirement plans and have taken a greater interest in the financial affairs of their families. Statistically, the female will live longer than the male and ultimately end up in charge of the family finances. Dual incomes have led to increased family wealth. The trap comes when the family expenses equal the income and then something unexpected happens that disrupts the income stream.

In relationships where one partner grew up with little concern for money because they had financially successful parents and the other had far less access to the benefits associated with wealth, there is a natural tension around money and how to spend it. Everyone needs to come to grips with the psychological drivers around money. Understanding these differences is part of the process that a couple can explore with their financial advisor as the wealth plan is being developed.

One of my classmates from school is a fourth-generation shareholder of one of the largest privately owned companies in the world. Her solution to dealing with the wealth bestowed on her was to go to law school, move to another city, and give away the majority of the inherited wealth. She was and is determined that she would not be defined by her good fortune and has made her own way in the world. Her cousins all have very different relationships with their inheritance. I am sure we all know people that inherited wealth that allowed them to make different choices. Unfortunately, research shows that inheriting generational wealth does not always turn out well because poor choices are frequently made.

There is an old saying,

"Shirtsleeves to shirtsleeves in three generations."

This refers to the first generation building wealth and the second generation spending it and the third generation... well, I think you get the idea.

This is even more true today because each generation over the past 100 years has lived longer than the previous generation. Longevity is expensive because people live longer in retirement, and those years eat away at financial assets that could be passed down. There are several strategies to mitigate the erosion of wealth with careful and thoughtful planning.

On the following page, take a few minutes to answer these fundamental questions about money and wealth:

In married families, each partner should answer these questions individually, then jointly discuss their answers.

Single individuals should also address these questions. The answers help guide everything else surrounding money and wealth in your life.

1. What does money mean to you?
2. Did you grow up in a family with an abundance or scarcity of money?
3. How does the answer to the above question influence your approach to money and wealth management?
4. How important is it to accumulate as much wealth as possible?
5. Are you interested in leaving financial assets to the next generation?
6. Are you interested in leaving money to charity?
7. Have you considered what your life will look like in retirement?

Families in the ultra-high net worth category tend to have family offices full of professional advisors that help manage their wealth. They recognize that it is in their best interest to have professionals on their team to guide them.

Most of us do not have the need or wealth required to have a dedicated family office. However, having a team of professionals quarterbacked by your financial advisor will accomplish the same thing at a fraction of the cost.

UNDERSTANDING RISK AND VOLATILITY

When we do risk profiles for our clients, we have each

partner do a profile. There is a good reason for both to take the risk profile before agreeing on a blended profile. Single investors also need to complete the profile. In both cases, discuss with your advisor.

1. Risk means different things to each of us.
2. Men and women typically view risk differently.
3. Volatility in stock and bond prices is constant and often confused with risk. Volatility is the price we pay for the long-term gains that the equity markets have delivered for the past 100 years.

> **According to Investopedia, "Risk is defined in financial terms as the chance that an outcome of an investment's actual gain will differ from an expected outcome or return. Risk involves the possibility of losing some or all of the original investment."**
>
> **Volatility is a measure of how much a stock's overall value fluctuates. (www.fool.com)**

Risk and volatility are often confused.

Additionally, advisors seldom discuss with investors the concept of the loss of purchasing power due to inflation. A conservative investment approach designed to eliminate volatility with fixed-income investments and alternative investments could very well lose the purchasing power of your money over time.

For example, buying certificates of deposit (CDs) and other relatively short fixed-income investments because the investor is guaranteed to get the principal back with interest will likely yield less than the rate of inflation. If you had done this 30 years ago when the wholesale price of gasoline was 78 cents per gallon and compared it today where the average wholesale price of gasoline is $2.69 and rising (2021), it would take four times as much interest from your bonds to buy one gallon of gas. Adding insult to injury, the yield on fixed-income investments has dropped from 10% in the 1980s to zero in 2008, and the rate continues to rest near zero 13 years later. Yet the price of gasoline has gone up four-fold.

It is important to understand the corrosive impacts of inflation on our lives and money. Investors need to have a clear understanding of the pros and cons of each investment instrument and find a strategy that provides growth greater than the rate of inflation. Your advisor should be able to find the right balance to fit your family's needs.

Often, one partner in a marriage is very risk-averse and wants to avoid any principal risk whatsoever. They feel that the money was hard to get and any loss is unacceptable. This is where it is important to understand the real risks of inflation—loss of purchasing power.

Another view is that taking reasonable risks/volatility is necessary in order to grow the value of the investments.

These differing views are a perfect example of the yin

and yang of the short-term versus long-term views of our lives. They also highlight the mental bias that individuals have toward risk/volatility.

The goal of financial planning is to find the right mix or balance of investments that have a strong probability of meeting the long-term goals for each family, not to beat the indexes or your neighbors' boastful returns.

In the early stages of financial planning, these viewpoints need to be reconciled so that the financial aspects of a couple's life do not ruin the marriage. Working through an in-depth discussion of risk can help couples find a happy medium.

Because capitalism is based on the idea of an ever-expanding world population and the economies of the world, the risk of total loss in the financial sectors is surely close to zero. There are periods of time that will test the resolve of investors, and many people make emotional choices that may hurt them financially in the long run.

One of the most important benefits of working with an advisor and having a well-designed plan is that, in trying times, your advisor can put her emotions into a box and use critical thinking skills and knowledge about her clients and the markets to guide you through the choppy waters of volatility.

In order to reduce the risk of loss, investors need to diversify their portfolios across several asset classes. Stocks, bonds, and real estate are the big three. Understanding how each asset class performs in various market conditions is also important to reduce risk.

One of the biggest hurdles to overcome for most people today is that their investment portfolios are updated in real-time—social media blasts us with daily or even hourly updates about markets rising and falling—and the fear and greed emotions kick in. Add to that the clickbait sites that claim secret "once in a lifetime investment opportunities" are available only to paying subscribers–a classic play on the emotions of greed.

For example, a client called one day because he was concerned that the market was going to drop for a while. I listened to his rationale, which was mostly driven by what he was seeing on his phone and what he heard from a friend who works at a mutual fund company. After I listened for a bit, I said, "John, that's all well and good, but you really aren't in the market. You happen to own shares in five world-class companies that you agreed are well run and good long-term investments. So you're not in the so-called market because you are an investor in companies with which you are familiar and are confident will grow over time."

I continued to remind him that his time horizon for these investments and investments in his retirement accounts were not the date he planned to retire but rather a 30-year time horizon. He understood, and we left the stock positions in place.

FEAR AND GREED DRIVE THE BUS

Understanding how you make decisions regarding investing will help you understand and evaluate investments and how they can work in your favor or against you.

We are all motivated by fear and greed, and this is clearly represented by how people manage their wealth, build their lifestyles, and view risk and reward.

Much of our understanding of risk is an emotional response, not a logical analysis. The ability to see risk for what it is, is an important component in managing wealth.

It is thought that the pain of losing is roughly twice as powerful as a successful outcome. "Losses loom larger than gains"[1] (Kahneman & Tversky, 1979). This explains why every time the stock market experiences a temporary setback, massive numbers of stocks are sold and the money moves quickly to money market funds or other safe investments. The fear factor has kicked in.

Greed is also the primary emotion that drives financial decisions, and as the markets rise, money flows back into stocks. This was evidenced in mid–2021 with GameStop shares rising from $17.25 a share on January 4 to $347.51 on January 27, and by August 7, 2021, falling back to $151.77. The stock rise was fueled by social media hype, despite the fact that the company was losing money and trying to restructure its business model to better reflect the current trends in the distribution of its products. This could be a multi-year process. Many people bought shares at considerably higher prices than the current price and have now experienced an unrealized or realized loss. These types of investments are speculative because they were made on an emotional basis rather than a fundamental basis.

> **TIP: Stock prices reflect what investors are willing to pay for future growth and profits, which elevate the value of the company and its shares over time.**

When we talk to clients, we like to reframe the concepts of risk of loss and the risks of losing purchasing power in the future. Risk of loss is a short-term emotional response that should be offset by the understanding that over the long term the only rational approach is to own financial assets that increase in value over time at a rate greater than the risk-free rate (currently close to zero) plus the rate of inflation.

The chart below is a 100-year chart of the Dow Jones Industrial Index, which represents 30 of the prominent industrial companies in the United States. As it climbs and drops over the years, it is perfectly clear that declines are short-term occurrences, and yes, they are hard to watch, but the long trend is up.

Source: https://www.macrotrends.net/1319/dow-jones-100-year-historical-chart

What is not to like about investing in assets that continue to climb? A closer inspection of the trend reveals that there has never been a ten-year time frame where the index was negative. The only question is how much it gained over the selected time frame.

Creating wealth is playing the long game. Managing wealth is a long game. Whether you are in the Accumulation Phase, Retirement Income Phase, or are fortunate enough to be in the multi-generational phase of wealth, the most important element is time invested. Start early, add often, and ... wait.

TIME HORIZONS MATTER

The longer the better. Accumulators tend to focus on retirement at age 65, but that is only half of the story. If you accumulate wealth for 40 years and then create an income for the rest of your life, let's say another 30 years, that is a 70-year time frame. If you are planning on passing assets to the next generation, we are now talking about over 100 years for one family. We have clients that are passing down wealth to the fourth generation. In the context of 70- or 100-year time frames and understanding the long-term upward bias to the capital markets, it is far easier to accumulate and build substantial wealth.

It is all about staying the course. Warren Buffett at age 90 is one of the richest men in the world, not because he is a better investor (although he is good) but because he started investing in his early 30s and made the bulk of his estimated net worth of $100 billion after the age of 65, even after giving away a considerable portion of his wealth. He invests in solid companies with terrific management teams in good businesses. He recently sold a significant portion of his Apple stock and reported in his annual shareholder letter that he considers selling the Apple position a mistake. He freely admits that he makes mistakes with his investments. The lesson from Buffett is to invest wisely and stay for the long haul.

Real estate investing is similar. Buy undeveloped land and hold it for a long time. Currently, multi-generation farms on the edges of expanding metropolitan areas are being sold for housing developments. The landowners are reaping decades of annual appreciation for the property and are benefiting from an expanding population that wants single-family homes in the exurbs.

PRIVATE BUSINESS WEALTH

The baby boomer generation that created and built privately owned businesses are looking at exit strategies to help them create liquidity. We work with exit strategy professionals to help these owners maximize the opportunities for a successful exit so they can move on to the retirement phase of their lives. Having a solid plan to optimize the exit and having an equally solid wealth management plan for post-exit go hand in hand. In many instances, a post-exit financial plan provides clarity to a business owner as decisions are made regarding timing and pricing. Many businesses have a board of directors to help the owner/CEO drive the business. Once you exit your business, it is wise to create a new "board of directors" to guide you through the next phase of your life.

For families and individuals that are concerned about building and preserving wealth, it is a good idea to expand the framework of how you think about wealth to include human and intellectual capital along with traditional financial capital. This refers to passing the wealth along to future generations in the family, which becomes more and more difficult with the expanding number of family members in the next generations.

Treating family wealth as a business entity with a mission statement, governance principles, and structure is a great first step for any family. Life throws us curve balls from time to time. Returning to the mission statement and structure helps guide families through challenging times. Working with your outside trusted advisors will help your family build a family-operating committee to drive decisions.

One of the families we are privileged to work with has a family foundation that grants funds each year to causes for which they feel strongly. They meet each year in a different location to reconnect as a family and make decisions about how they will disburse the funds to organizations that embody the values of the family.

The first generation has passed away and the second generation of family members are now in their 90s and have passed the torch to their children. The third generation, in their 60s, have been part of the annual meetings for a number of years and recently have taken over the allocation process. Soon the fourth-generation family members will be invited to participate in the process, preparing them for the time when they will lead the family foundation.

You may think only ultra-wealthy families engage in this type of activity, but many families have set aside funds to help their communities and involve their children and grandchildren in the process to teach them about philanthropy. Donor-advised foundations facilitate this process so each family does not have to create a private foundation with the expenses and restrictions imposed on family foundations.

UNDERSTANDING WALL STREET: WHERE MONEY IS BORN

The investment banks in the world play a critical role in the financing and funding of companies as they start off small and grow. Growth takes capital (money) to add employees, develop products, build manufacturing facilities, and fuel the engine of our global economies. Companies utilize Wall Street firms that are willing to raise investment capital for them. The capital could consist of venture capital and eventually shares of publicly traded stock or bonds in a company. There is an important distinction between the two types of investments.

BONDS

Companies, municipalities, state governments, quasi-governmental agencies, and the US government are examples of entities that issue bonds. Bonds are essentially a debt instrument that typically has a fixed maturity date and a promise to pay interest periodically or at maturity. As an investor who buys a bond, you are essentially loaning the money in exchange for interest payments. CDs are essentially a form of bond that banks issue to savers. The more secure the entity is perceived to be, the lower the rate investors receive. Short-term treasury bills, which are guaranteed by the US government, pay the lowest rate. As the length of time until maturity increases, the rate investors receive is typically higher. As the risk of the issuing entity is perceived to be greater, the rate that investors receive is also higher as a reward for taking on the additional risk of default by the issuer. Companies issue bonds/debt and pay interest rather than selling more ownership (equity/stocks) in the company.

STOCK

Owning stock is essentially becoming an owner of the company. For example, when an investor buys shares in Apple, they can reap the benefits as the company grows and expands, resulting in the share price appreciating.

Another way to think of this is: As a shareholder of stock in a company like Apple, every day 147,000 employees get up and go to work for you as an owner/shareholder. Or if you own shares in Microsoft, 144,000 employees go to work every day for you as an owner/shareholder.

Naturally, you are only one of the thousands of shareholders along with many of the employees at publicly traded companies that you have invested in by purchasing common stock shares. The difference is that, as a shareholder, you simply own the shares without having to manage the company or make any decisions on the day-to-day operations. Talk about leverage; owning shares in public companies is tremendous leverage of your time and energy to pursue your life while your investment grows over time.

STOCKS OR BONDS: WHICH IS BETTER?

The answer to this question depends on the objective of the investment. The first level of decision would be, are you interested in growth or just income? As an investor looking for just income, the bonds could be a good choice. But it is important to understand that the upside potential is capped on the yield of the bond and the downside risk is 100% of the investment in the event the company fails or they mature and return your principal. If the rates have fallen, your new return, if you choose to buy new bonds, could be quite a bit lower. Bond yields are typically in the low single-digit levels depending on length until maturity and interest from corporate bonds are taxable. Municipal bonds are tax-free and normally yield less than corporate bonds.

An investor that wants growth and is willing to accept price volatility over time would certainly want to own stocks rather than bonds. There will be times when your equity portfolio has declined due to volatility. Bonds also have price volatility, especially in the current low-rate environment that will at some point move higher, creating volatility for owners of fixed-rate bonds.

Returning to the example of Apple, the stock has appreciated by 284,000% since the late 1980s. In contrast, had you purchased bonds issued by Apple during the same time frame, your returns would have been less than 8% annually. A clearer picture of this is to look at the past five years ending in mid–2021. The stock price has returned 442.26%. The bonds are less than 5% a year or a combined 25% over five years.

To be fair, not all or even very many publicly traded companies are as successful as Apple. However, the example illustrates the difference between being an owner of a company and loaning money to a company through the purchase of bonds. Bonds will pay a steady return over time, whereas stocks will experience periods of flat or negative growth along with the upside growth. Knowing this is important if you want to be a good long-term investor.

HOW IT WORKS BEHIND THE SCENES

Wall Street understands the psychological implications of investors as they react to changing investment climates and economic and political cycles. To be clear, Wall Street is a product-manufacturing industry that designs products to play on both sides of the fear–greed emotional roller coaster many people experience. As an investor, you should ignore the constant barrage of "investment tips" that flood social media, television programming touting some strategy or another, and even talk radio professing that the world is about to collapse and you need to own (fill in the blank).

As financial advisors, we lock these emotions into a

proverbial box and look at the data using critical thinking skills acquired over many years to develop wealth plans and strategies to help achieve the desired results. Removing the emotional aspect of investing is key to long-term success.

There is one other important concept that I want to share with you—Modern Portfolio Theory (MPT). This is important because most financial products (alternative investments included) are created to fit into the model to build an ideal portfolio based on risk and return assumptions for each asset class in a portfolio and then match to the client risk profile.

MPT was introduced by Harry Markowitz in a 1952 essay.

> **"Modern portfolio theory is a mathematical framework for assembling a portfolio of assets such that the expected return is maximized for a given level of risk. It is a formalization and extension of diversification in investing, the idea that owning different kinds of financial assets is less risky than only one type. Its key insight is that an asset's risk and return should not be assessed by itself, but by how it attributes to a portfolio's overall risk and return. It uses the variance of asset prices as a proxy for risk."**

When the MPT was introduced, the financial markets were far less complicated than they are today. In the 1950s, 60s, and 70s all the way up until the early 2000s, bond yields, which were an important part of the theory, ranged between 4%–6% on average. In the early 1980s, interest rates spiked almost to 20% for a short period of time. Interest rates spent the next 30 years dropping to virtually 0%, which culminated in 2008.

The bond or fixed income component of the theory was an important part in reducing volatility or what some folks would call risk in the portfolio. The problem today is that portfolios holding 20%, 30%, or even 40% in fixed-income bond investments have little or no return, and the theory no longer applies.

Not to be undaunted, the Wall Street product machinery created a myriad of products that supposedly reduce portfolio risk and volatility. The problem with this is that it doesn't address the real issue: investors incorrectly perceive volatility in the short term as a bad occurrence. Markets fluctuate, and when portfolios are down in value, which happens frequently, investors feel like they have lost money. The truth is, they have not lost any money unless they sell, which will then lock in the loss. In fact, history suggests that when markets are down, it is the best time to invest to take advantage of acquiring more shares at lower prices. Americans love a bargain!

To illustrate this point, we look to Peter Lynch, who managed the Fidelity Magellan fund from 1977 to 1990.

> *"Under his management, the fund averaged an astounding annual return of 29%, while the annualized S&P 500 return during that time was 7.43%, while the average Magellan fund investor earned only 5.96% or less."* [2]

You might ask, how could this be? The answer is quite simple, and it goes back to the perception of risk versus volatility. Unfortunately, investors left to their own devices have a high propensity to buy high and sell low because emotions drive their decisions. This is one more reason to have an advisor with decades of experience who can guide you through the various cycles of the markets. It's also extremely important that the investment portfolio is created after a comprehensive investment management plan is developed for each family and investor. What's good for one investor or family will be different from the next one.

Ironically, most professionals in the industry acknowledge that the risks today in the fixed income/bond markets are equally as great as the rewards were for the 30 years prior to 2008. In other words, when interest rates rise again, as they surely will, bond prices will fall in value significantly. Bonds with longer maturities that are not held to maturity could lose significant percentages of their investment principal in these fixed-income securities.

As a result of this situation, bond managers and investors are choosing ultra-short-duration bond funds to hedge against the risk. The problem here is that, after fees, taxes, and adjusting for inflation, the real return on these "safe assets" is negative. This means that even though all of the invested principal is returned, the dollars will purchase fewer goods and services because of inflation. This is a recipe for running out of money at some point in the future when you can least afford it.

Negative or zero returns on a large percentage of an

investment portfolio is acceptable for the short term. In 2008, when the Federal Reserve lowered rates to effectively zero, it was inconceivable that this would last very long, and soon rates would rise moderately again.

As I write this in May 2022, short-term rates are still below 1% and the ten-year treasury yield is roughly 3%. Although the yields have increased from a year ago, they are still far below the official rate of inflation estimated to be near 8%. Owning fixed income assets continues to reward investors with negative rates of return.

Using the MPT model of asset allocation, which is baked into most financial planning programs, portfolio returns will be muted in the short term, and long-term outcomes may be impacted depending on how many more years bond yields remain low. Hopefully, you understand that owning high-quality stocks is the best choice for financial investors who want to build wealth over time.

In the current environment, how should a portfolio be invested? The answer depends on the goals, time horizons, and needs of each investor. An experienced, qualified financial advisor can make a huge difference in your long-term outcomes. I will provide some ideas about this later in the book.

THOUGHTFUL PLANNING COMBINED WITH APPROPRIATE RISK-ADJUSTED ASSET MANAGEMENT

WHEN EMOTIONS OVERRIDE THE ADVICE AND PLAN

Bill and his wife Anne were referred to me by a mutual acquaintance. Bill's sister had recently passed away and had left just over $1 million to him, all in an IRA. This case was tricky partly because the assets were all pre-tax.

We met several times, and they expressed their desire to sell their home in the Twin Cities and build a new home on a lake in northern Minnesota. Bill decided to retire from his job supervising maintenance crews for a large organization in St. Paul.

I was a little concerned about what they wanted to do because of the tax consequences of withdrawing money from the IRA and building a new home, which often exceeds the budget. In addition, they owned a condo in South Carolina where they spent the winter months.

We discussed the potential issues of concentrating on real estate rather than having a diversified portfolio of stocks and bonds along with some real estate.

Things went well for several years until Bill and his wife called because they wanted to buy a second condo jointly with their daughter. The rationale was that the condos could be rented in the off-season, which would cover most of the expenses of owning the properties.

I was skeptical of this plan because they would have three properties that all had mortgages, and I knew that the daughter had limited income. My advice to Bill and his wife was that they do not buy the second condo. We had several conversations about it; however, they were insistent that they knew what they were doing.

They bought the second condo in 2006, and when the economy took a significant drop in 2008, they discovered that they had more debt on the condos than they were worth, and they were not attracting enough renters. They ended up losing money every month on the two condos.

Every month, they would call to take money out of their IRA accounts to cover the cost of the mortgages on their three homes. They listed both condos for sale and sold the bigger one first, which netted them a small profit. The second condo sold six months later at a loss.

Unfortunately, Bill and his wife continued to take monthly distributions from the IRA account and their small amount of savings until it became evident the Bill would have to go back to work at 65 years old.

Being creative, Bill was able to find ways to make money reselling products on the internet, which he continues to do today.

As advisors, we can only do so much. In hindsight, the purchase of the second condo crippled their financial picture so much they couldn't recover. I did the best I could to outline the downside risks of cutting their finances so tight that an economic downturn would take them down with it. Little did I know that the downturn was only two years away.

The lesson in this story is that one major benefit of having a wealth management advisor is that they can prevent you from making big mistakes.

OVERVIEW OF WEALTH CREATION

In a capitalist society like the United States, wealth is created through several different avenues, but essentially, they are all related. Capital formation is at the heart of building wealth and the three primary avenues are real estate, private business ownership, and ownership of shares in publicly traded companies.

These are all related because they all take capital investment, daily management, and a long-time horizon to maximize investment returns. Most people do not have enough capital to start a business nor the ability to borrow enough capital. They prefer to work for companies that have the structure and capital to thrive and grow.

One of the important elements in creating wealth is leverage. Leverage exists by growing a business enterprise by hiring employees and continually expanding the business.

The owners of a business have leverage because they do not have to make every product or item that is sold. Owners assume the risks of acquiring capital and running the business, which includes hiring employees to convert capital (money) and raw materials into finished goods. In the software industries and other tech businesses, capital is required to hire engineers to develop the intellectual products, and it can take many years before any sales occur.

In the case of real estate, such as farmland, the family uses the land and builds leverage through technology, improved crop management, and decades of ownership. Because of the advanced technologies, the average size of a farm continues to grow as consolidation occurs and average annual yields increase due to better farming practice. The ownership of rental real estate leverage comes from the rents paid that service the debt used to build the properties. The owners create internal wealth as the mortgages are paid by tenants and properties appreciate in value over time.

In a similar way, private business holders can also expand their business over time by adding employees to do the work, adding new products and services, investing in new facilities and equipment, and managing the overall operation of the company. Owning a company is not an easy endeavor, and not many people are suited for it or able to raise the capital and manage the business successfully. Those that do can pass the companies to the upcoming generations or sell the companies to new owners.

The third category is to own shares of publicly traded businesses and participate in the success or failure of the business. The big advantage is that your leverage consists of all the people that work for the company essentially on your behalf. A great example of this leverage is that if you own shares in Microsoft, every day 166,475 people go to work on behalf of the owners and themselves. By owning shares in several large and successful companies that continue to grow over time, even small investors can benefit from the success and financial gains these companies achieve with their shareholders. There are so many examples of highly successful companies about which we know. It would not be a stretch to suggest that many of these companies have made our lives easier, better, and more interesting. Yes, the founders of these companies have made billions of dollars in personal wealth, but the investors in these companies have also made an equal amount of wealth just distributed over a wider number of people who invested in these companies.

SECTION 3:
PULLING IT ALL TOGETHER

FINDING THE RIGHT ADVISOR: EXPERIENCE AND RESOURCES MATTER

As you move from the Accumulation Phase to the Retirement Income phase of your financial life, it is critical that you have prepared emotionally and financially before retiring or selling your business. The Retirement Income phase is much more complicated than the Accumulation Phase and considers the additional income streams from Social Security, pensions, deferred compensation stock options, if any, and your investment portfolio.

> One way to think of this is: we all have a family doctor to guide us until we make a transition or have a health occurrence that requires more specialized training. In the case of business owners looking to exit, several specialists are

> **required to ensure that owners maximize the after-tax results. Different specialists are required to help manage and optimize the Retirement Phase and begin to plan for the final asset transition phase.**

There are many small advisor firms that offer investment, tax, and estate planning services; however, they offer a basic level of service in each area whether clients need it or not. There is also usually an extra charge for the additional services, which is fair. The issue is determining whether you need those services.

A better model is to hire a highly qualified and experienced financial advisor team that has decades of experience working with families like yours. In addition to years of experience, some advisors have taken the time and energy to continue their education by getting advanced industry designations that focus on the needs of HNW families. Your advisor team should include at least two advisors that are from different generations, and if possible one should be female. Statistically, females live longer than their male partners and will most likely be in charge of the family finances at some point. Additionally, we have learned that female advisors connect in a different way with female clients, engaging them in the process throughout the years.

You may want to consider a team of at least one advisor that has an advanced industry education designation that focuses on the areas of need you will encounter. For HNW families, an advisor with a CPWA® designation is a great choice. This designation program focuses on the specific issues of HNW families.

According to www.finra.com, there are currently 212 designations that advisors in the financial industry can qualify for by passing examinations. Most designations also require annual ongoing education in the specific areas of the industry, including ethics training.

These designations are offered by independent organizations and can be broad in nature or specific. One of the broadest is the Certified Financial Planner CFP® offered by the College of Financial Planning. The curriculum is extremely broad and offers an introductory knowledge base of many parts of the industry, many of which are not applicable to the typical affluent and HNW family needing financial advice. There are close to 90,000 CFP designation holders in the country. In addition, there are minimal industry experience requirements to become a CFP. In fact, many firms encourage non-advisor staff to take the curriculum for designation. Some of the large advisory firms include the CFP program in their new advisor training. There are also specific designations that focus on narrow topics like pension funds and employee benefits.

Over the years, I have been designated as an Accredited Investment Fiduciary®, Accredited Wealth Manager™ (only offered to employees of a former firm), and Certified Investment Manager®. All of these were useful at the time. As I began working with HNW families, I determined that the Certified Private Wealth Advisor (CPWA) designation was the perfect fit for my clients' needs. The designation course work deepens the knowledge base needed to effectively serve the many HNW family issues.

Designations matter because you know that your advisor has expertise in the areas that apply to your needs. There are currently only about 3,000 CPWA® in the country because of the depth of knowledge and industry experience required to qualify, and most advisors are focused on affluent families with different needs than HNW families.

To be fair, these designations do not qualify financial advisors in the areas of taxation or estate planning. Each of those areas needs qualified specialists. The advanced education from designation programs helps advisors know when to call in the experts that specialize in taxation and estate planning because they are extremely complex and technical areas.

In our practice, we have access to internal tax, estate, and trust company specialists to review and recommend actions that a client should consider if necessary. We also partner with outside lawyers and tax experts that are specialists in their fields. We work together as a team on behalf of our clients. Each outside expert charges only for the work that they do. There are no referral fees or quid-pro-quo deals.

This is important to us because you should only pay for services you need. Typically the estate planning services and tax services are needed only occasionally, so there is no need to pay fees for those services on an ongoing basis. Estate plans should be reviewed as the tax laws change or every five years as needed.

We had a client a few years ago that assured us that they had their own attorney draft an estate plan for them. We took them at their word, and a few years ago we equally divided shares of low-cost basis stock into single accounts for each of them. The plan was that when the first one died, the step-up in cost basis would eliminate the capital gains tax. When the first spouse passed, we asked for a copy of the will to move the stock shares to an estate account and then to the surviving spouse on the stepped-up cost basis. When we received the documents, it turns out that they were drafted 25 years earlier by their company corporate attorney and an accountant named as co-trustees. The attorney had since passed away and the accountant retired many years ago. What could have been a simple transfer of assets became much more complicated and needed to go to probate court, which takes time and additional expense. The attorney did not specialize in estate planning.

> **The lesson in this is to be sure all estate planning documents are current with existing tax laws and designed correctly to minimize costs and delays at the time of passing for each spouse.**

We require our HNW clients to provide copies of these documents for our review and to add to their file. We have our internal partners review them to ensure the documents are appropriate under current laws. If we see items that are concerning, we recommend that their documents be updated. We do not charge a fee for this service.

There is one other reason you should have independent

professionals take care of your taxes and estate planning documents rather than captive professionals in an investment firm or company. It is important to separate these functions to obtain the best advice for your family. Eliminating conflicts of interest will ensure you get the right advice.

> **Your financial advisor should ideally be dual-licensed with Series 7 and Series 66 licenses. This allows an advisor to access a far wider approach to investments besides mutual funds and managed accounts.**

The investment industry has a wide variety of investment options to choose from, and new products come out every day. To manage the continuous offerings, many investment companies limit what products their advisors can offer. Advisors with a Series 65 license can only offer open-end mutual funds that most people are accustomed to buying and managed account portfolios. Many firms that are only registered investment advisors are included in the restricted offerings.

As advisors with Series 7 and 66 licenses, we are eligible to offer any investment products, including individual bonds and stocks outside the constraints of mutual funds and managed accounts. The chapter Common Sense Investment Strategies will go deeper into the rationale and benefits of various types of investment approaches.

Serious advisors have a standard of care that outlines the services that will be provided on an ongoing basis to ensure that you are on track to meet your goals. They should be able to provide a list of services that are typically provided in each of the four phases. As we age and our wealth increases, we likely will need more services to help in the complex stages of decline and asset transfer. A sample list is included in the Appendix.

A few final thoughts regarding the choice of a financial advisor. As in so many professions, experience matters. A surgeon with 30 years of knee reconstructions would be preferable to one with five years. Finding the right team of advisors is essential for all members of your family, in the current generation and the next. Think of your team of advisors as your board of directors, and your financial advisor, by virtue of ongoing reviews, the one you will have the most frequent contact with should be seen as the chairman of the board.

Our job advising HNW families through their Accumulation Phase or handling their post-exit phase after the sale of their company or hard assets requires specialized knowledge that comes through years, even decades, of experience.

Many advisors have little experience with bear markets because the last one was 2008, and before that 2001–2003. We have experienced the "lost decade" of 1999–2009, recessions in the early 1990s, and the major bear markets of 1987. We understand market cycles and how to react to them because, as they say, "this is not our first rodeo."

> **Like airline pilots, when the sky is blue and markets climb, experience matters less. When markets correct or the airplane loses an engine, you want the best, most qualified pilot/advisor at the controls to guide you home safely.**

Lastly, we recommend that families work with advisors they like and trust. Friends and acquaintances are not always the best choice, especially when the markets are performing poorly or your family is facing a challenge of some sort.

When I first came into the business, we were advised, "Do not do business with your family because there might come a time when you need a hot meal and a warm place to sleep." In recent years, we have been asked by extended family members to oversee their plan and have agreed to do so with an understanding of expected services and commitments to follow our advice.

Being a financial advisor involves business relationships with individual families that trust us to guard and grow their family wealth. We need to get it right, which means sometimes making tough calls to protect our clients' interests.

> **OUR GOAL IS TO ENSURE OUR CLIENTS DO NOT MAKE BIG MISTAKES**
> **We Solve Problems for Clients, Including Investment, Tax, and Estate Problems**

INVESTING IS THE VEHICLE TO REACH YOUR GOALS

Just like your car or an airplane are the vehicles to transport you to your destinations, investments and planning are the vehicles to deliver you to the **time** in your life when you meet or exceed your goals.

This is where investor behaviors matter the most. Even if you have done all the right things regarding your finances, handling the investment part is where many people fail because they fall victim to their own emotions. Psychologists tell us that we experience the pain of loss to a much greater degree than the joy of success.

The investment process is the one aspect of wealth management that typically gets all the attention. Every day, consumers' emotions are appealed to in order to motivate them to take action. Earlier in the book, I talked about fear and greed. Unfortunately, fear sells, and Wall Street understands this bias and is happy to provide products to ease your fears.

When I attend investment education and product conferences, the primary discussions are around limiting volatility and reducing risk (volatility) with products designed to make you feel better. The problem is that when you limit volatility (perceived risk) by adding complicated "if–when" conditions, guaranteed minimum returns, and hedge funds designed to buffer downside, you often limit upside potential.

The truth is that all sorts of investment asset classes work well in some environments and not as well in others. The problem is we do not know in advance which asset classes will perform better than others in a given period of time.

For years, we have used the Annual Asset Class Returns chart which shows the annual return and ranking for each asset class.

We show this to new clients and ask them to take a good look at it and tell us what the pattern is. You should try it now. With a quick Google search, you can find the most updated version.

The typical answer we get is that they do not see a pattern but maybe it's a trick. They are partially right in so much as there is no pattern. What's in favor today or last year may very well be out of favor next year. It's even more interesting to look at the range of returns annually for each asset class ranked from best to worst and then look at one or two of the asset classes and how they have fared in the previous ten years.

Typically what happens is when one asset class performs really well, the money starts flowing to it even though it may fall out of favor in the near future. The nice people who sell these products are busy emailing and calling financial advisors to tell them why the client should own their product now.

Here's a shocker for you—the fund representatives never call or email us to tell us that we should move the money out of their fund and into another asset class. That's up to each advisor to decide. In 2020 and early 2021, companies that manage value funds, which have been thrashed by growth funds for a number of years, started calling because value stocks overall had one good quarter where they outperform growth. One quarter does not warrant any changes, and a well-designed portfolio rarely needs changes except for periodic rebalancing.

The point of this exercise is that investors and advisors are in no position to predict future performance in any of the asset classes. The only rational solution is to invest your money in several of the asset classes so that you can take advantage of different asset classes and the rotation of funds currently in favor. It doesn't mean the other ones are going to be miserable in performance; it's just a prudent thing to do as you progress toward meeting your goals.

> **"Everything should be made as simple as possible but not simpler." —Albert Einstein**

ACTIVE VS. PASSIVE INVESTING
OPEN-END ACTIVELY MANAGED MUTUAL FUNDS

The next important topic around investing is active vs. passive investment management. For decades, open-ended actively managed mutual funds dominated the industry and served investors well.

Here is how open-ended funds operate. At the end of every trading day, the fund managers value all of the stocks or bonds in the fund, review the redemptions and the new money additions, deduct their fees and trading expenses, and come up with a new daily value called **Net Asset Value**.

In an actively managed fund, there is a team of professional analysts who research stocks and the economy before deciding on how much of each stock or bond it should buy or sell in order for the fund to balance and deliver a competitive rate of return against an index and the benchmark asset class peer group.

Every mutual fund is actually an investment company. It is governed by a prospectus that outlines the objectives of the fund and has limitations on maximum exposure by industry type and limitations on individual positions in any security it owns on your behalf. These guidelines protect investors and guide the managers.

Going back three decades in reviewing mutual fund prospectuses, the cost of participating in those funds was anywhere from 3%–5% annually. That expense drags on performance. Today's actively managed open-end funds have costs under 1% in most instances. Fees across the industry have fallen considerably since the mid–1900s. That is good for investors.

PASSIVE INDEX FUNDS

In 1975, Vanguard Funds was founded to take advantage of offering mutual funds with significantly lower cost structures than the actively managed funds. They did this by offering funds that matched the indexes like the S&P 500 fund. No need for research associates, salespeople, or costly trading costs.

Vanguard was a frontrunner in driving the costs lower and triggered the entire industry to compete by lowering the cost of their investment products.

Initially, these no-load funds were not available to financial advisors because there was no compensation element to pay the advisors or their firms. As the internet appeared in the 1990s, the no-load industry exploded, and investors could buy and sell funds with little or no cost.

The dialogue for a couple of decades was that investors did not need to pay an advisor and should just buy indexed funds because most (not all) open-ended managed funds underperformed the index funds. There is some truth to that statement. Approximately 60% of active mutual funds indeed do not meet or exceed the benchmark index funds. So the idea is to look for active funds that have a long track record of outperforming their index over a 3-, 5-, or 10-year period of time and low turnover. Your advisor can find them.

If you consider the S&P 500 fund, which has 500

stocks, the return is the average of the performance of those 500 companies. As averages work out, the bottom half of the companies, about 250 of them, actually hurt the performance for investors. Add to that that the index is capitalization-weighted. This means that the top companies by size impact the index significantly in rising and falling markets and typically consist of 20 or fewer companies. So if that is true (it is), why would you own shares in the rest of the companies?

This approach has been extremely successful for Vanguard and other similar no-load, low-cost index funds. Ironically, John Bogel, founder of Vanguard, conceded a few years ago that investors were better served by using the services of a financial advisor to help with investment selections and allocations.

Which is better?

$3,879,601 ✱
The Growth Fund of America

$2,570,017
AMCAP Fund

$1,390,347
Washington Mutual Investors Fund

$1,358,033
The Investment Company of America

$1,280,481 ✱
S&P 500 Index[a]

$1,193,894
American Mutual Fund

1976 1980 1984 1988 1992 1996 2000 2004 2008 2012 2016 2020

[a]The market index is unmanaged and, therefore, has no expenses. Investors cannot invest directly in an index.
Source: Capital Group

The chart on the previous page from American Funds compares their four actively managed equity funds against the S&P index fund. Pay particular attention to the years of 1999 through 2009. Also pay attention to the accumulated value of a $10,000 investment from start to 2020.

I think it is safe to say that the discussion is over. Quality active management is vastly superior to index funds over long periods of time. According to Global Insights, 17.49% of actively managed funds outperform the S&P 500 over a ten-year time frame as of June 30, 2021. Your advisor should be able to help you find the 17% that have historically outperformed the S&P 500 index.

These seemingly small items add up to big differences over time. The choice ultimately is yours. The outcomes will also be yours.

Investing in a low-cost index fund assures you 100% of the upside with less fees and 100% of the downside and fees. The example above illustrates how active management can outperform on the downside by limiting the volatility somewhat, and when the markets return to an upward bias you are starting from a point ahead of the index investors. Because the active managers are not restricted to the index and its stock weighting, they do not own the worst-performing stocks in the index, which gives them a big advantage when the markets recover.

EXCHANGE-TRADED FUNDS (ETFS)

Exchange-traded funds (ETFs) are the latest entry into the fund offerings. You can trade them many times during a day as opposed to open-ended funds where trades are processed at the end of every day for the new orders to buy and orders to sell.

One big advantage over open-ended mutual funds is tax management. When you add an ETF to your portfolio, you are getting current pricing and no embedded capital gains or losses like you would with open-ended funds.

Another advantage of ETFs is that their cost structures are even lower than actively managed mutual funds and, in some cases, even the open-ended index funds.

Some ETFs are also actively managed, which increases their costs. The current trends show a persistent and increasing flow of funds from actively managed funds toward the ETF platforms, both index and now more actively managed ETFs. Many of the active fund managers are also offering ETF actively managed funds, which are a great addition to client portfolios.

SEPARATELY MANAGED ACCOUNTS (SMAS)

Separately managed accounts (SMAS) are also an incredibly viable approach to managing the equity portion of your investment portfolio. Essentially, these are accounts managed within a specific asset class, like large-cap growth, and the manager will have a model portfolio with the individual securities showing up in the client accounts.

This approach will typically result in clients owning only the stocks that the manager has currently placed on the buy list. The advantage is that there are no embedded capital gains that might happen with mutual funds. As the manager makes some changes in the model portfolio, the client portfolio will change accordingly. This process allows for greater transparency of the actual holdings for the client and advisor to see, and it allows for tax management each year as appropriate. Another advantage of SMAs during periods of volatility is that you avoid the tax issues when mutual funds are experiencing outflows by investors selling. This creates potentially taxable capital gains distributions to the fund investors in a year when the total return of the fund may also be in negative territory. With an SMA structure, you are not subjected to the taxable gains each year from the need to create liquidity for other investors.

Another characteristic of SMAs is that they typically hold far fewer positions than the broad-based indexes and, as a result, have the opportunity to be more reactive and nimble when they are trying to liquidate or establish new positions.

The discussion regarding active vs. passive investment products is a smoke screen to the central issue because **investor behavior** matters far more than actual investment performance. A diversified asset allocation plan will account for 90% of the return, with the final 10% dependent on **investor behavior**. Therefore, we stand firm in managing our clients' behaviors regarding their choices and emotions.

As clients, you may have concerns and thoughts about your investments, the economy, and overall progress toward your goals. Regular and honest conversations between advisor and client is a critical component to a successful advisor–client relationship.

VALUE PROPOSITION OF HIRING AN ADVISOR

I have been making the case that hiring a top-notch experienced advisor is in your best interest. Below are three estimates of the average annual added return for investors who use an advisor, as researched by Envestnet, Russell Investments, and Vanguard Funds. These studies used different methodologies and are long-term focused. The 3% average additional return cited below is calculated after an average 1% annual advisor fee and will vary depending on the firm and the client's needs.

What they do not take into consideration is the tax planning and estate planning processes that top-notch advisors implement for their clients along with other professional advisors in those fields. You can find these studies on the Fidelity website at the bottom of the section "Why Work with a Financial Advisor." www.fidelity.com

The value of advice sources:

> **Envestnet, Capital Sigma:** The Advisor Advantage estimates advisor value adds an average of 3% per year.
> **Russell Investments** estimates an advisor adds about 4% per year.
> **Vanguard study (2019)** estimates lifetime value adds an average of 3% annually.

The methodologies for these studies vary greatly. The Envestnet and Russell studies sought to identify the absolute value of a set of services, while the Vanguard study compared the expected impact of advisor practices to a hypothetical best-case scenario.

The calculations are pretty simple for illustration purposes.

$1,000,000 with a 6% return for 25 years equals $4,483,896 before taxes—all dividends and capital gains reinvested.

$1,000,000 with 9% return for 25 years equals $8,919,553 before taxes—all dividends and capital gains reinvested.

This is pretty compelling. Even if you do not have $1 million and are simply growing your investment portfolio with pre-tax accounts, Roth IRAs, and after-tax investments, it makes sense to get the best returns possible in an appropriately allocated portfolio.

ELIMINATING EMOTIONAL DECISIONS AROUND MONEY CAN SAVE PORTFOLIOS

How do you know which advisor to hire? Here is a checklist and some thoughts about who you want on your team.

1. How long has your advisor been in the industry? Longer is better, and 20 years of experience should be a minimum. In the case of a team, at least one advisor should have several decades of experience.
2. Your advisor team should include at least one woman and should ideally be multi-generational.
3. Is the advisor dual-licensed? Can he/she offer

packaged investment solutions and investment strategies of individual stocks and bonds?

4. Does the firm offer fee-based solutions along with commission accounts for assets that do not need ongoing management?

5. Do the advisor and firm have an agnostic investment solution platform, or are they confined to what their firm offers?

6. What type of designations does your advisor hold, and are they focused on your needs? Are they CPWA® or CFP® certified?

7. How many households does the advisor service? 100 or less is ideal.

8. How often will you meet with your advisor? Quarterly, semi-annually, or annually?

9. Do you like the advisor(s)? You are entering into an important long-term business relationship.

10. Do you have shared values and interests with the advisor(s)?

11. Do you trust your advisor(s)?

12. See the Standard of Care template in the Appendix.

RED FLAGS:

1. High-pressure sales tactics

2. Advisors who dominate the conversations and do not make the time to understand your particular situation and needs

3. A quick handoff to staff
4. A rush to additional services from the firm that could result in additional charges
5. Advisors who charge an annual fee for financial plans and asset charges for advice unless a specific agreement is in place for advanced planning for a fee
6. Frequent recommendations that are not in sync with the financial plan and stated goals and objectives
7. Recommendations for products that you do not understand
8. A lack of transparency

It is important to think of your financial advisor like other professionals in your life. They do not need to be in your friend circle any more than your CPA, attorney, or dentist. They need to be your trusted advisor.

We work with people we like and trust to be good partners in this important journey.

Make a list of your current advisors and coaches in your life:

Here is a list to consider, and you can add your own.

- CPA/tax accountant
- Estate planning attorney
- Corporate attorney
- Strength trainer
- Massage therapist
- Personal grooming specialist

- Business marketing specialist
- Business planning specialist
- Leadership mentor or coach
- Chiropractor
- Orthopedic doctor/oncologist
- Fishing and hunting guide
- Hosted trip guide
- Family physician
- Medical specialist
- Travel planner
- Personal executive assistant
- Horse or dog trainer
- Book editor and advisor ☺
- Publicist
- Guitar teacher (my favorite)
- Sports coach
- Landscape professional

All of these and more fit into the category of short or near term service providers. Many you use only once a year or maybe every five years. They all require that you pay them for services, and we are happy to do so.

Hiring a financial planner is a long-term engagement that can help you grow and protect your family's wealth for several generations. You should have frequent conversations with your trusted financial advisor several times a year or more often as the circumstances dictate. The better your planner knows you and your family, the better outcomes you should expect to achieve.

"We all hire experts and professionals in our lives to make ourselves better, our lives more efficient, and activities more productive. Expert advisors and coaches allow each of us to focus on our strengths and expertise."

FOLLOW THE MONEY

There is a saying I heard while working for a large Wall Street firm in the early part of my career that goes like this: "In every transaction, there are three participants—the client, the firm, and the advisor. If two out of three win, it'll be a good day."

With the limited partnership mania in the '80s and annuities and high yield (junk) bonds in the '80s and '90s, many alternative investments and products were manufactured and sold to clients to appeal to their fears that all fall into the category that only two of the three will win. You can guess which two win every day.

When I hear that xyz product is their best selling product, I head for the door. If they say "only for your best, most sophisticated clients," I advise you to run for the door, too.

Long-term wealth is created by ownership of companies that are profitable and grow over many years. Companies that are well managed and profitable and invest the profits appropriately to ensure a fair return to the owners (shareholders) and retain profits to reinvest and grow the company are good candidates for investors.

DIVERSIFICATION OR DE-WORSEIFICATION?

We have all heard the phrase, "Do not put all of your eggs in one basket." But what does this mean?

- Buy mutual funds, maybe the same ones, at different companies?
- Buy index funds and managed funds in the same category, which essentially creates a great deal of overlap?

Neither choice accomplishes the goal of diversification.

Diversification in its purest form spreads the risk of excess loss at the portfolio level by owning a broad range of investments that are not correlated to each other.

Modern portfolio theory (MPT) is based on the idea that markets are efficient, and a mix of asset classes diversifies the holdings by investing in non-correlated assets. The theory says that giving broad exposure to different investments in the United States and across the world is the best approach to managing risk and return.

The problem with this theory is that neither assumption is accurate. Markets are not efficient, and investors are not always rational.

For simplicity, think of stocks vs. bonds. Typically, they

will not track each other in volatile markets, and when some assets are not performing well, others may be doing just fine. Even different asset classes of stocks will come into and out of favor over time.

During periods when the market has significant draw-downs, many non-correlated assets behave exactly like the traditional stock/bond portfolios.

As the number of stocks increases in the portfolio, it becomes less diversified. Think about the S&P 500 example. Because the return is the average of the 500 individual stocks, it works out that the bottom 250 perform worse than the top 250. So why own shares in the bottom 250 companies? Because more is not better. It is average.

If a portfolio includes several mutual funds, it is possible to end up owning virtually all of the stocks available in the markets.

We recently reviewed a proposal for a foundation that had 16 mutual funds recommended between stocks, bonds, and money market funds.

Ten of the mutual funds/ETFs combined own 10,000 stocks, and the top holdings in each fund appear in at least three other funds in the portfolio. This is, in my analysis, de-worsification of the portfolio and, frankly, overweighting the portfolio unknowingly.

Also, be careful of under-diversification. Investors often concentrate their wealth into one or two companies for a variety of reasons, mostly emotional. The truth is that no company lasts forever.

During the financial crisis of 2008, many of the

employees of major investment companies had invested their retirement dollars in their own company stock. Almost overnight, wealth built over many decades disappeared as their company failed. Imagine what that felt like for those employees and their families. This has happened frequently over the years. Many companies now limit how much of the company stock employees may own in their retirement funds.

Be diversified, not deworsified.

NOISE, NOISE, AND MORE NOISE

Every day, we are bombarded with financial news that evokes emotions intended to encourage or discourage us and results in our taking some sort of action. The problem with taking action is transaction costs, taxes, and a change in the investment plan.

I know of an investor who sold all of his investments when Barack Obama was elected president because he didn't like the new president. That individual is still in cash, having missed over 14 years of great market returns.

Recently, a client told me that most of her friends had gone to cash when President Biden was elected president because they didn't think the economy would do well and that the market would crash. Of course, there is no evidence to support this idea and the markets have risen to new levels.

These are symptoms of mixing politics and investing.

In fact, equity markets typically do better under Democratic administrations until they do not. History tells us not to mix politics with investing.

From 1977 through 1990, the Fidelity Magellan growth fund managed by Peter Lynch had an average annual return of just over 29.2% a year. During that same time, the average investor in that fund lost money, according to Fidelity. Shocking to say the least. This is a classic buy-high-sell-low mistake made by far too many investors.

More recently, Charlie Munger, Warren Buffet's partner in Berkshire Hathaway, said,

> **"The first rule of compounding is not to interrupt it unnecessarily."**

With a combined estimated net worth of 103 billion dollars, this philosophy seems to have worked for these two gentlemen.

With the right mindset and proper asset allocation, any investor can have a good rate of return over the long term. Because humans are emotional and complicated, it is always useful to have a good advisor at your side to help you understand how wealth accumulation works and to make sure you don't make big mistakes.

POLITICS, THE FED, AND FISCAL POLICY

It would not be fair to ignore these three things when thinking about wealth management issues and investing. Since the 2008 financial crisis, the Federal Reserve Bank (the Fed) has been a major player in the economy, triggered by the situation in the real estate and mortgage industry. Several financial firms collapsed, were sold, or were bailed out by the Federal Reserve bank. In doing so, the Fed provided the liquidity required for the banks to survive.

The Fed is considered the lender of last resort when other solutions are not viable in times of crises. In calmer times, the Fed has a mandate from Congress to manage the economy toward full employment and keep inflation in check. The idea is that, with full employment and a robust economy, inflation should average around 2% a year.

After the 2008 liquidity crisis and financial market correction, economic collapse was averted by reducing interest rates to virtually 0% and the Fed buying trillions of dollars of bonds from banks in exchange for cash. The thought was that the economy would rebound, employment would recover, and interest rates would return to normal.

What happened was that employment grew substantially along with the economy, but long-term interest rates remained quite low for a variety of reasons outside the control of the Fed. This was a new experience for the Fed, and inflation has remained stubbornly below the Fed target of 2% for the past 16 years. This scenario did not fit into the generally accepted economic theories that had been in place for decades.

Fast forward to the 2019 pandemic and the government-mandated lockdown of the nonessential economy. With the focus on fighting the COVID-19 virus, the Fed was again forced to provide massive amounts of money to keep the country afloat. Once again, the Fed came to the rescue, but without a playbook. We all know what happened in 2021 regarding restarting the economy, vaccines, and the stubbornly slow return to work.

Presently, in the fourth quarter of 2021, short-term interest rates remain near zero and mortgage rates have fallen well below 3%, fueling rising real estate values and home buying. In addition, cheap money has flowed into the stock market, which some claim has inflated the value of stocks. All of this is likely true, but it is far more complex, and the cause and effect relationships are hard to prove in all cases. Corporate earnings (profits) continue to increase significantly, exceeding analysts' expectations, which we know directly correlates to what investors are willing to pay for the shares.

Politics and fiscal policy are determined by Congress and the Executive branch, and the Fed executes those policies within the limited tools that exist—short-term interest rate targets and bond purchases—to ensure adequate funds are in the banking system to fuel the economy. Currently, the Fed is reducing their bond purchases, and the expectations are for somewhat higher short-term rates over the next couple of years. The impact is not known; however, the markets have likely priced these changes into equity values already.

The Fed is designed to be a non-political entity; however, the connection between fiscal policy and politics is evident, especially in the years preceding national elections.

COMMON SENSE INVESTMENT STRATEGIES

After creating your overall financial plan, the next step is to establish an asset allocation approach to ensure that you have created a diversified (but not over- or under diversified) portfolio.

The idea is to use cost-efficient platforms and utilize asset managers that perform well in up and down markets. This is called **capture ratios.** The goal is to capture close to the benchmark index return for each manager on the upside and better (less drawdown) than the index benchmark on the downside, thereby starting in a stronger position when the markets resume their upwards moves.

ASSET CLASSES

Companies are grouped based on their individual enterprise value, which is the number of shares outstanding multiplied by the current share price. Additionally, company life cycles help determine whether a company is primarily a growth company or a value company (more mature and often dividend paying). Cap is shorthand for capital valuation.

1. Large-Cap Growth—US (such as Amazon and Apple)
2. Large-Cap Value—US (such as 3M and General Mills)
3. Mid-Cap Blend—US (Some companies fall between growth and value)
4. Small-cap growth—US
5. International/developing markets
6. Fixed income, if needed

A starting approach would be to allocate a percentage to fixed income and equal percentages to the other five asset classes and rebalance once a year back to equal weighting. The fixed income percentage depends on the age of the client and anticipated needs for liquidity in the next several years.

Using historical risk and return metrics for each asset class, we sometimes will overweight the large-cap growth and value segments in order to reduce some of the volatility in the portfolio if that is desired. Again, this is determined after several conversations with clients about their experience and knowledge of financial markets and the long-term goals they have established.

The next step is investing in each category to build what we call an **all-weather portfolio** that will perform well in up markets and down markets without the market timing and tinkering that often occurs as markets fluctuate. Refer back to the example of the Magellan Fund from the chapter Noise, Noise, and More Noise.

Using what we learned in previous chapters, the ideal approach is to use separate account managers for the large-cap (company) segment and the mid-cap blend segment because they typically hold far fewer positions in the portfolio and therefore are more nimble, allowing them to react to changing market conditions quickly.

The small-cap area typically needs a broader base of investments, and good active mutual funds or ETFs can be a good choice in this segment.

The international and developing markets are best accessed by using actively managed SMAs, mutual funds, or ETFs. These markets represent close to 70% of the world stock markets and take a very specialized approach. In some cases, we will use several managers to ensure we are getting adequate geographic diversification.

If a fixed-income component is part of the plan, utilizing a commission-based account to build a bond ladder is oftentimes the best solution. With this approach, you have the opportunity to pay a small percentage when you purchase the bonds, and there's no ongoing annual fee. Be sure your advisor has experience in the fixed-income area and access to an institutional bond desk to help build out your portfolio of fixed-income securities. The only ongoing fees would occur when bonds mature and replacement bonds are purchased. The fees are only charged on the purchase, not on maturities.

As you look at this sample asset allocation model, you will notice there are no index funds. As we discussed in earlier chapters, index funds provide an average return on all of the securities that are held in the index. Many of the companies that are included in the indexes actually detract from potential return.

Even if you do not have enough financial assets to access SMAs, the same principles apply. Many firms like ours offer research-based solutions with the diversification required to meet the objectives.

If most of your financial assets are in your employer pre-tax retirement plans, your advisor should be able to help you identify which funds you should be looking at that will approximate what you are trying to accomplish with a proper amount of diversification.

Because no one knows where the markets are heading in the short term and understanding the need to adequately diversify the portfolio to meet the long-term goals of each family, this approach provides the structure needed to achieve good results in up markets and down markets by focusing on the best companies in the world, not all of the companies.

A reasonable expectation for your portfolio is that it will perform well in up markets consistent with applicable benchmarks without owning the indexes and that it will outperform the indexes when the markets are not performing well. This is the **secret sauce** to improving long-term outcomes for your family.

Historically, the equity markets have returned 7% to 8% annually over long periods of time. There are periods of time, like the past couple years, where equity returns have been two or three times higher than the historical average. There will also be times when the returns are quite a bit lower than the long-term averages. A long-term focus will help avoid making bad decisions in the short term.

When building your financial plan for retirement, you should model equity returns in the 6% or 7% range to be conservative. Over the past 20 years, returns have actually been somewhat higher. If your plan has a high projected success rate based on all of the inputs, you should be able to sleep well in all market cycles. If your plan barely meets your projected needs in retirement, it would be a good idea to return to the expense side of the plan and adjust your contributions to your investment accounts.

In our practice, we strive to have plans that have an 80% or better chance of success with the Monte Carlo simulation based on current inputs. Of course, things change over time, so we continue to update the plan and monitor the long-term projections to make sure that we are on track. The plans are living documents updated constantly and reviewed with clients at least annually or more often as needed.

Market corrections, when stocks go down in value for a while, occur on a regular basis. In fact, some sort of pullback is expected each year. Then the market recovers and resumes moving higher. In late 2021, we have not had a correction since March of 2020, and the pundits suggest we are overdue. I do not pretend to know if they are right any more than they can predict where the markets are going. At some point, a recession and lower-equity values will occur as they have fairly regularly for the past 100 years. Once recessions end, the markets will resume trending higher.

Understanding the logic of the unpredictability of market movements in the short term leads us to the inevitable realization that staying the course with a beautifully constructed portfolio that covers numerous asset classes is the only rational course of action.

The financial media negative marketing machine will do their best to scare you into believing that the world is coming to an end, again, and you should buy gold, crypto, pork bellies, real estate, insurance policies, and God knows whatever else they are selling. Today I saw two clickbait messages screaming about a "once-in-a-generation, go-all-in buy recommendation" and three similar ads touting the end of the financial world as we know it. To learn more all I have to do is pay them some money to hear about these amazing opportunities. Probability suggests they are both wrong. They understand the psychology of money and people, and they are playing to your fears and greed. Ignore them.

> **"A fool and his money are soon parted." This phrase dates back to the book of Proverbs 21:20 King James Bible. It is certainly relevant in modern times as well.**

Tune them out and call your advisor if your advisor has not called you recently. If you cannot get a hold of your advisor, call us. We will help you make sense of whatever the markets are doing that worries you.

TIME HORIZONS

Time horizons matter, and the longer your time horizon, the easier it is to absorb the occasional drawdowns in prices and asset values to take advantage of the long-term benefits. Most of us think short term. We plan for our next vacation, graduations, weddings, and other life events that are easy for us to think about. Remember the analogy of planning for a destination instead of planning for a time in our lives?

> **Manage your family wealth with a 100-year time horizon and you will make better choices and worry less about the short-term volatility in the markets and life.**

As an industry, we feed the short-term perspective beast and report quarterly returns, which are somewhat important, but families should really be thinking of time horizons greater than 100 years.

What? 100 years? I think it is safe to say that most of us have relatives approaching 100 years old, and the experts are suggesting our children/grandchildren will live beyond 100 years.

We all have apps on our phones to track our investments by the second and let us know that xyz has underperformed the market for the last 24 hours. Wow, that is completely useless information. Put into that perspective, the short-term "over and under" average annual performances will blend into long-term wealth accumulation.

The implications are that portfolios not only need to be managed to support the increased longevity, but asset transfers will occur 20–30 years later than they did in the previous generations. This means individual investors need to go on their own until they potentially inherit assets in their 70s and 80s instead of 50s and 60s.

CRYPTO CURRENCIES, GOLD, AND OTHER STUFF

We get asked about crypto currencies as investments quite often. It is hard for us to comment specifically because they are so new and have no legal standing as a currency. It will take some time, if it ever happens, for the current banking world to adapt to digital payments and maintain the pricing stability needed for widespread acceptance.

Additionally, we are racing forward into a digital world where cryptocurrencies may have a role as the younger generations continue to embrace alternative systems of their financial lives. Crypto is just one piece of the evolving world we are living in with mass migration; reimagined ways of living; and working in the face of global climate change, environmental challenges, and rapidly advancing technologies that transcend current national boundaries and political systems.*

In the same general context, the Federal Reserve is exploring the idea of digitizing the dollar. This will be a complex process that will take several years to accomplish. Other nations are also exploring this approach.

I believe we will all learn a great deal more about these blockchain-enabled systems and digitized currencies in the coming years.

WHAT DRIVES CHANGES IN THE PRICE OF GOLD?

Over the past several decades, the price of gold has been influenced by many different factors. Gold's price history has seen some significant ups and downs, and dramatic changes in price may be fueled by such issues as central bank buying, inflation, geopolitics, monetary policy, equity markets, and more.

One of the biggest drivers of gold is currency values. Because gold is denominated in dollars, the greenback can significantly impact the price of gold. A weaker dollar makes gold relatively less expensive for foreign buyers and thus may lift prices. On the other hand, a stronger dollar makes gold relatively more expensive for foreign buyers, thus possibly depressing prices. Fiat, or paper currencies, tends to lose value over time. If this continues to be the case, gold could potentially continue in an uptrend as investors look

---

*   See resources

to it for its perceived safety and potential as a hedge against declining currency values.[3]

The problem with owning lots of gold is that the price movements are unpredictable. Owning the physical commodity can be expensive to store and hard to convert back to dollars in the time of need. The best answer to the question about gold that I have heard is, "Gold makes beautiful jewelry."

Back to the question about gold, other nontraditional investments, and Crypto. If you feel a need to own some of these assets, keep the percentage of your portfolio committed to them to the low single digits. That way, you can tell your friends you are participating and have fun tracking them. The same would hold true for highly speculative meme stocks that captured people's imagination and money in the spring and summer of 2021. We do not recommend allocations of these assets to our clients' portfolios.

ALTERNATIVE INVESTMENTS
AND STRUCTURED PRODUCTS

This category is broad, but it has a couple of consistent themes.

1. Claim to reduce volatility
2. Link several products or strategies together to create new products
3. Typically have some sort of research and trading strategy that has worked for a while
4. Charge an ongoing annual fee or 2%
5. Often take a 20% incentive fee on the profits each calendar quarter as values go up
6. Usually have little or no transparency of the investment strategy or holdings
7. Use limited liquidity or gates to keep the clients in the investment

8. Use leverage or derivatives to enhance returns that also can crush the investment when things go wrong

Based on what we learned so far, these are classic fear and greed investments. They were very popular with the Ivy League college endowments for many years until things changed and they fell out of favor. The consistent winners are the investment managers because they get paid very well when times are good, and if the strategy falls out of favor, they close the fund and start a new one so they do not have the hurdle of previous high values before earning their incentive fees.

Some of these investments are pretty good, but understanding them is a challenge. Over the past 25 years of handling client accounts that had these investments bought at other firms, none have worked out. A couple broke even after a few years so we were thankful for the return of the money. However, in most circumstances, the clients lost money. Lost money is hard to recover from.

If your advisor cannot explain to you how these work, then avoid them and stick to your plan around equities and bonds.

FOCUS ON WHAT YOU CAN CONTROL

With all of the information I have shared, perhaps the most important point is that to be successful as an investor, you have to believe in the long-term wealth creation opportunities offered by the equity markets to all investors.

Your outcomes will be determined by your behaviors as an investor even more than which fund or stocks you pick or which asset managers you hire. Market timing, speculating, chasing last year's winners, falling prey to your emotions, and trying to enter or exit markets based on your feelings is not investing.

Here are the things you can control:

1. Decide what your goals are regarding retirement funding and/or family life transitions.
2. Create a plan to achieve your goals.

3. Be persistent with funding your plan and stay with it through the ups and downs of market cycles.
4. Work with a great financial advisor to help guide you and keep you on track.

If you are fortunate to have accumulated considerable wealth so that your retirement years are assured, then consider doing the following:

1. Thank your lucky stars for the lifetime of financial success you have experienced.
2. Educate your children and grandchildren about how to be successful investors instead of spenders of their money and eventually yours.
3. Work with your financial, tax, and legal advisors to plan for multi-generation stewardship of the assets that reflect your values and ethics.
4. Create a family foundation to give back to a world that needs help.

As I mentioned earlier in the book, retirement is a time in your life, not a predetermined place or age at which you arrive.

The origins of the concept of retirement from work go back to the 18th century as government policy. In the mid-1800s, certain US municipal employees started receiving pensions. In the 1920s, a variety of private industries began offering pensions. The thinking at that time was that workers were less effective, took more time off, and were sick more often after the age of 40. Skipping forward to the present day, the Mental Health Foundation estimates that one in five retirees experience depression and declining health. So what gives?

- I have worked with retiring clients, and within a year many of them are back at some sort of work that they care about. They thrive in their retirement years.
- I have also had clients who retired and never returned to work, nor did they have any hobbies or activities that gave them purpose. They seemed to age quickly and became focused on their health issues because they did not have much else to think about.

It is also important to remember that life expectancy has nearly doubled since the early 1900s, yet the notion of retiring and living a life of leisure continues. Additionally, work in those days was mostly physical, whereas in today's world, most work is intellectual and takes a lesser toll on our health. Actually, our intellectual capital increases every year with experience.

Research on brain plasticity has shown that staying engaged, continuing to be challenged intellectually, being curious about the world, and learning new skills delay the onset of dementia and Alzheimer's.

The majority of this book centers on the first part of the journey, which is accumulating enough wealth so that you can choose how you live in retirement. We have learned over the years that individuals who have a purpose in life, regardless of whether or not they are getting paid, seem to have happier and healthier years after their official retirement.

Many individuals work well into their 70s because they love their work. They may scale back, but they stay engaged. Many take up new careers or volunteer for nonprofit organizations for which they are passionate. They may also have several hobbies that they like to pursue that they did not have the time to do when working full time.

My personal hobbies include coaching hockey in the winter, photography, fly fishing, downhill skiing, and recently, taking up the electric guitar and writing this book. Adding to that, I volunteer on the local planning commission and serve on a couple of nonprofit boards. When I am with my friend/leadership coach, we remark that our lives are full, and we like it that way.

Instead of thinking about retirement as the end of work at a specific age, think of retirement as a transition into a new way of staying engaged in life, pursuing causes and activities that you are passionate about and give you purpose.

I recently heard about a fellow who retired and was so excited that he got to play golf every day. After about six months, his golf game was worse than before he retired. He realized that golf (insert your favorite hobby) was a pleasurable break from his job. Now golf is his job, and he is miserable.

CONCLUSION

Now that you have a better understanding of the wealth accumulation, management, and stewardship of the family wealth process, what are your next steps?

STACK THE DECK IN YOUR FAVOR:

- With an understanding of the four phases of wealth management throughout your lifetime, you can begin to plan for success, regardless of which phase you enter into the process.
- For corporate employees with company-sponsored retirement plans, be sure to utilize them to the fullest if possible. If not, make a plan to set aside retirement funds every paycheck and follow the advice in previous chapters.
- For those in the gig economy or in small business environments that do not have corporate plans,

create your own with a Solo 401(k) profit-sharing plan or SEP (Simplified Employer Plan) IRA that allows for matching funds from your own business as well as contributions from your income. You definitely need a financial advisor and a good accountant to get this right.

- For those of you selling a business, planning for your next chapter of life is critical to achieving the **Freedom of Choice** you have worked so hard for your entire life. Find a great financial advisor for pre-exit planning who can help you plan for your post-exit life.
- For those who are converting family assets like farmland or commercial real estate that have been in the family for several generations, you also need a great team of advisors around you who will help you take the next steps with the newfound wealth.
- Entrepreneurs with new wealth also need help before and after the liquidity events.

ADVISOR CHECKLIST

- At least one team member with a minimum of 20 years of experience
- Multi-generational team with at least one female advisor
- Series 7 and Series 65 licensed advisors
- A firm with an open architecture that offers a broad range of platforms and options

- A firm that has a strong reputation in the industry, not just the biggest firms. Firms with up to a couple of thousand advisors across the country tend to be more client-focused and substantial enough to ensure that the client experience meets regulatory requirements while being able to provide custom solutions for each client as needed.
- Ability to access top money managers through SMAs, mutual funds/ETFs, and individual stocks and bonds
- Advanced industry designations, such as a CPWA® Certified Private Wealth Advisor

Build a team of advisors around you with the financial advisor as the quarterback or chairman of your family board of advisors.

If your current advisor does not have access to an open platform with SMAs and individual stock and bonds, you might have outgrown your advisor. You will want to consider getting a second opinion from an advisor team that meets the qualifications above.

If you hold several alternative investments (hedge funds, structured products, whole life insurance), definitely get a second opinion.

If you do not have an advisor, you need one if you want to have a worry-free retirement with freedom of choice.

We provide second opinions frequently. Many of our clients come to us this way. It is a risk-free way to get to know each other and see if there is a mutual fit for a business relationship. Either way, you will benefit from the experience.

SIX KEYS TO A SUCCESSFUL RETIREMENT

1. Have a plan of what you want to do and how you are going to pay for it.
2. Find activities that give you a sense of purpose.
3. Stay engaged socially.
4. Keep moving to ensure you are healthy. Consider hiring a personal trainer that focuses on functional movement and balance along with strength training.
5. Eat well and take care of your body.
6. **Remain positive and grateful for all that you have accomplished in your life.**

Talk through these issues with your family and your financial advisor. Together you can craft a plan to live with purpose in your retirement years and have the freedom of choice to do so.

ABOUT THE AUTHOR

HAL TEARSE has been a financial advisor since 1976, holding several management positions in that time. Since entering the financial services industry, Hal has continued his education through advanced training programs and seminars. He is a past member of the NASD Board of Arbitrators and he earned his Bachelor of Fine Arts in journalism and mass communication from the University of Minnesota.

Hal formed the Tearse Wright Group in 2018 when he welcomed his partner, NICOLE WRIGHT. Together, they partner with their clients on all aspects of their financial lives and goals. This team approach allows for more support and service to the families that they serve.

Investing in his community has always been a priority for Hal. Having served on numerous boards and committees, he has spent time and resources to help further the causes he strongly believes in.

Hockey has been a part of Hal's life for as long as he can remember. After suffering an injury in college, he did not want to walk away from the game – as a natural leader, he became a coach. His passion for hockey and his desire to help develop players both on and off the ice has been an instrumental part of his life.

Hal resides in Minnesota with his wife, Lynn, and he has two children. He is an accomplished photographer whose award-winning photos have been featured around the world. Hal also enjoys fly fishing, skiing and playing guitar.

GLOSSARY OF TERMS

Every profession has its own language that can be hard for individuals outside the profession to understand. It is also common for the professional to present information using the jargon of the industry. Hopefully the explanations below will help you decipher the language.

Comprehensive wealth management involves the combined services of the legal, accounting, and investment management professions. Each discipline has its own jargon and role in creating, managing, and protecting family wealth.

WHAT IS A CPWA®?

Certified Private Wealth Advisor® (CPWA®) is an advanced professional certification for advisors who serve high-net-worth clients. It's designed for seasoned professionals who seek the latest, most advanced knowledge and techniques to address the sophisticated needs of clients with a minimum net worth of $5 million. Unlike credentials that focus specifically on investing or financial planning, the CPWA® program takes a holistic and multidisciplinary approach.

WHAT IS THE S&P 500 INDEX?

The S&P 500 Index, or the Standard & Poor's 500 Index, is a market-capitalization-weighted index of the 500 largest publicly traded companies in the United States. It is not an exact list of the top 500 U.S. companies by market capitalization because there are other criteria included in the index. The index is widely regarded as the best gauge of large-cap U.S. equities. Other common U.S. stock market benchmarks include the Dow Jones Industrial Average, or Dow 30, and the Russell 2000 Index,[4] which represents the small-cap index.

WHAT IS THE DOW JONES INDUSTRIAL AVERAGE (DJIA)?

The Dow Jones Industrial Average (DJIA), also known as the Dow 30, is a stock market index that tracks 30 large, publicly-owned blue-chip[5] companies trading on the New York Stock Exchange and the NASDAQ. The Dow Jones is named after Charles Dow, who created the index in 1896 along with his business partner Edward Jones.

The DJIA is the second oldest US market index; the first was the Dow Jones Transportation Average.[6]

The DJIA was designed to serve as a proxy for the health of the broader US economy.

WHAT IS A STOCK?

A stock (also known as equity) is a security that represents the ownership of a fraction of a corporation.[7] This entitles the owner of the stock to a proportion of the corporation's assets[8] and profits equal to how much stock they own. Units of stock are called "shares."

Stocks are bought and sold predominantly on stock exchanges, though there can be private sales as well, and are the foundation of many individual investors' portfolios. These transactions must conform to government regulations, which are meant to protect investors from fraudulent practices. Historically, they have outperformed most other investments over the long run.[9]

WHAT IS AN INDEX FUND?

An index fund is a type of mutual fund or exchange-traded fund (ETF)[10] with a portfolio constructed to match or track the components of a financial market index,[11] such as the Standard & Poor's 500 Index (S&P 500).[12] An index mutual fund is said to provide broad market exposure, low operating expenses, and low portfolio turnover. These funds follow their benchmark index[13] regardless of the state of the markets.

WHAT IS A MUTUAL FUND?

A mutual fund is a type of financial vehicle made up of a pool of money collected from many investors to invest in securities like stocks, bonds, money market instruments, and other assets. Mutual funds are operated by professional money managers,[14] who allocate the fund's assets and attempt to produce capital gains or income for the fund's investors. A mutual fund's portfolio is structured and maintained to match the investment objectives stated in its prospectus.

Mutual funds give small or individual investors access to professionally managed portfolios of equities, bonds, and other securities. Each shareholder, therefore, participates proportionally in the gains or losses of the fund. Mutual funds invest in a vast number of securities, and performance is usually tracked as the change in the total market cap[15] of the fund—derived by the aggregating performance of the underlying investments.

WHAT IS A BOND?

A bond is a fixed-income instrument[16] that represents a loan made by an investor to a borrower (typically corporate or governmental). A bond could be thought of as an I.O.U.[17] between the lender[18] and borrower that includes the details of the loan and its payments. Bonds are used by companies, municipalities, states, and sovereign governments to finance projects and operations. Owners of bonds are debtholders, or creditors, of the issuer.

Bond details include the end date when the principal[19] of the loan is due to be paid to the bond owner and usually include the terms for variable[20] or fixed-interest[21] payments made by the borrower.

KEY TAKEAWAYS

- Bonds are units of corporate debt issued by companies and securitized as tradable assets.
- A bond is referred to as a fixed-income instrument because bonds traditionally paid a fixed interest rate (coupon) to debtholders. Variable or floating interest rates are also quite common.
- Bond prices are inversely correlated with interest rates: when rates go up, bond prices fall and vice-versa.
- Bonds have maturity dates, at which point the principal amount must be paid back in full or risk default.

WHAT IS A MONTE CARLO SIMULATION?

Monte Carlo simulations are used to model the probability of different outcomes in a process that cannot easily be predicted due to the intervention of random variables.[22] It is a technique used to understand the impact of risk and uncertainty in prediction and forecasting models.

WHAT IS CRYPTOCURRENCY?

A cryptocurrency is a digital or virtual currency[23] that is secured by cryptography, which makes it nearly impossible to counterfeit or double-spend. Many cryptocurrencies are decentralized networks based on blockchain[24] technology—a distributed ledger enforced by a disparate network of computers. A defining feature of cryptocurrencies is that they are generally not issued by any central authority, rendering them theoretically immune to government interference or manipulation.

WHAT IS A HEDGE FUND?

Hedge funds are actively managed investment pools whose managers use a wide range of strategies, often including buying with borrowed money and trading esoteric assets, in an effort to beat average investment returns for their clients. They are considered risky alternative investment choices.

Hedge funds require a high minimum investment or net worth, excluding all but wealthy clients.

KEY TAKEAWAYS

- Hedge funds are actively managed alternative investments that typically use non-traditional and risky investment strategies or asset classes.
- Hedge funds charge much higher fees than conventional investment funds and require high minimum deposits.
- The number of hedge funds has been growing by approximately 2.5% over the past five years, but they remain controversial.
- Hedge funds were celebrated for their market-

beating performances in the 1990s and early 2000s, but many have underperformed since the financial crisis of 2007-2008, especially after fees and taxes are factored in.

- Getting to them is easy, but getting out of them is extremely difficult, thus locking you into the investment and the firm selling it to you for many years.

WHAT IS AN ALTERNATIVE INVESTMENT?

An alternative investment is a financial asset that does not fall into one of the conventional investment categories. Conventional categories include stocks, bonds, and cash. Alternative investments include private equity or venture capital, hedge funds, managed futures, art and antiques, commodities, and derivatives contracts. Real estate is also often classified as an alternative investment depending on how it is packaged.

WHAT IS COMPOUND INTEREST?

Compound interest (or compounding interest) is the interest on a loan or deposit calculated based on both the initial principal and the accumulated interest from previous periods. Thought to have originated in 17th-century Italy, compound interest can be thought of as "interest on interest," and will make a sum grow at a faster rate than simple interest,[25] which is calculated only on the principal amount.

The rate at which compound interest accrues depends on the frequency of compounding, such that the higher the number of compounding[26] periods, the greater the compound interest.

Sad, but true.

> **1-800-GoodLuck – The number used when trying to call a call center at any of the large financial entities to discuss your investments.**

WHAT IS A 401(k) PLAN?

The 401(k) plan was designed by Congress to encourage Americans to save for retirement. Among the benefits they offer is tax savings.

There are two main options, each with distinct tax advantages:

- A traditional 401(k) is deducted from the employee's gross income. The employee's taxable income is reduced by that amount and can be reported as a tax deduction for that year. No taxes are due on the money paid in or the profits it earns until the employee withdraws it, usually after retiring.
- A Roth 401(k) is deducted from the employee's after-tax income. The employee is paying income taxes on that money immediately. When the money is withdrawn during retirement, no additional taxes are due on the employee's contribution or the profits it earned over the years.

WHAT IS A 403(b) PLAN?

The 403(b) plan is similar to its better-known cousin, the 401(k) plan.[27] Each offers employees a tax-advantaged[28] way to save for retirement, but investment choices are often more limited in a 403(b), and 401(k)s serve private-sector employees.

The features and advantages of a 403(b) plan are largely similar to those found in a 401(k) plan. Both have the same basic contribution limits: $19,500 in 2020 and 2021.[29] The combination of employee and employer contributions are limited to the lesser of $58,000 in 2021 (up from $57,000 in 2020) or 100% of the employee's most recent yearly salary.[30]

OUR STANDARD OF CARE CPWA®

Investments & Wealth Institute members, candidates in Institute's certification programs, and Institute certificants ("Institute professionals") are required to adhere to the following principles:

1. Act in the best interest of the client.
2. Disclose services to be offered and provided, related charges, and compensation.
3. Disclose the existence of actual, potential, and/or perceived conflicts of interest and relevant financial relationships, direct and/or indirect. Take appropriate action to resolve or manage any such conflicts.
4. Provide clients the information needed to make informed decisions.

5. Respond to client inquiries and instructions appropriately, promptly, completely, and truthfully.

6. Maintain confidentiality of client information, however acquired, consistent with legal and regulatory requirements and firm policies.

7. Provide competent service by truthful representation of competency, maintenance and/or development of professional capabilities, and, when appropriate, the recommendation of other professionals.

8. Comply with legal and regulatory requirements related to one's practice of his or her profession.

THE FEDERAL RESERVE EXPLAINED

The 11th edition of *The Fed Explained: What the Central Bank Does* (formerly *The Federal Reserve System Purposes & Functions*) details the structure, responsibilities, and work of the US central banking system. The Federal Reserve System performs five functions to promote the effective operation of the US economy and, more generally, to serve the public interest. It includes three key entities: the Board of Governors, 12 Federal Reserve Banks, and the Federal Open Market Committee.

1. **Overview of the Federal Reserve System**[31]
   The Federal Reserve performs five key functions in the public interest to promote the health of

the U.S. economy and the stability of the U.S. financial system.

2. **The Three Key System Entities**[32]
   The Board of Governors, the Federal Reserve Banks, and the Federal Open Market Committee work together to promote the health of the U.S. economy and the stability of the U.S. financial system.

3. **Conducting Monetary Policy**[33]
   The Federal Reserve sets U.S. monetary policy to promote maximum employment and stable prices in the U.S. economy.

4. **Promoting Financial System Stability**[34]
   The Federal Reserve monitors financial system risks and engages at home and abroad to help ensure the system supports a healthy economy for U.S. households, communities, and businesses.

5. **Supervising and Regulating Financial Institutions and Activities**[35]
   The Federal Reserve promotes the safety and soundness of individual financial institutions and monitors their impact on the financial system as a whole.

6. **Fostering Payment and Settlement System Safety and Efficiency**[36]
   The Federal Reserve works to promote a safe, efficient, and accessible system for U.S. dollar transactions.

7. **Promoting Consumer Protection and Community Development**[37]

The Federal Reserve advances supervision, community reinvestment, and research to improve understanding of the impacts of financial services policies and practices on consumers and communities.

BIBLIOGRAPHY

This bibliography lists resources that have influenced the ideas and thoughts presented in this book. A couple are focused on the changing shifts of power and influence in the global economy driven by demographics, Global Warming, and increasing migration. Some make a strong case for owning equities over any other asset classes. A few address the current economics of our country.

Simple Wealth, Inevitable Wealth by Nick Murray www.nickmurray.com Nick is a 50-year veteran of the investment industry and tells it like it is. He provides common sense advice about wealth accumulation and the value of an advisor.

Calafia Beach Pundi; Scott Grannis. Scott is unique in the investment/economics world because he is not selling any products. He retired after several years as an economist at Western Asset Management. His views are fact- and data-based and quite interesting. www. scottgrannis.blogspot.com

Morningstar.com for mutual fund information

Family Wealth—Keeping in the Family by James E. Hughes Jr. How Family Members *and* Their Advisors Preserve Human, Intellectual, and Financial Assets *for* Generations

Investopedia www.investopedia.com A great resource to find definitions about complicated financial terms and platforms. Definitions above provided by Investopedia.

Move; The Forces Uprooting US by **Parag Khanna**. A compelling look at the powerful global forces that will cause billions of us to move geographically over the next decades, ushering in an area of radical change.

Brian Wesbury — 101 Brian is an economist at First Trust, and he says he is the *"Antidote to Conventional Wisdom"* (my type of guy!). He writes posts weekly and posts videos about the economy. https://www.ftportfolios. com/retail/blogs/economics/index.aspx

Stocks for the Long Run is a book on investing by Jeremy Siegel.[38] According to Pablo Galarza of *Money*, "His 1994 book *Stocks for the Long Run* sealed the conventional wisdom that most of us should be in the stock market."[39] James K. Glassman, a financial columnist for The Washington Post, called it one of the ten best investment books of all time.[40]

The Psychology of Money: The Timeless Lessons on Wealth, Greed, and Happiness by Morgan Housel

The Accidental Superpower: The Next Generation of American Preeminence and the Coming Global Disorder By Peter Zeihan

Thank you for investing your valuable time to read this book. We are always available for your comments.

Contact us at:

TEARSE WRIGHT GROUP
www.tearsewrightgroup.com
htearse@rwbaird.com
newright@rwbaird.com
888-831-6426 toll free
952-249-7630

ENDNOTES

1   https://www.jstor.org/stable/1914185

2   https://www.forbes.com/sites/forbesfinancecouncil/2021/06/02/
how-investors-are-costing-themselves-money/?sh=23baf3985e30

3   goldprice.org

4   https://www.investopedia.com/terms/r/russell2000.asp

5   https://www.investopedia.com/terms/b/bluechip.asp

6   https://www.investopedia.com/terms/d/djta.asp

7   https://www.investopedia.com/terms/c/corporation.asp

8   https://www.investopedia.com/terms/c/core-assets.asp

9   https://www.investopedia.com/terms/l/longrun.asp

10   https://www.investopedia.com/terms/e/etf.asp

11   https://www.investopedia.com/terms/m/marketindex.asp

12   https://www.investopedia.com/terms/s/sp.asp

13   https://www.investopedia.com/terms/i/index.asp

14   https://www.investopedia.com/terms/m/moneymanager.asp

15   https://www.investopedia.com/terms/m/marketcapitalization.asp

16   https://www.investopedia.com/terms/f/fixed-incomesecurity.asp

17   https://www.investopedia.com/terms/i/iou.asp

18   https://www.investopedia.com/terms/l/lender.asp

19   https://www.investopedia.com/terms/p/principal.asp

20   https://www.investopedia.com/terms/v/variableinterestrate.asp

21   https://www.investopedia.com/terms/f/fixedinterestrate.asp

22   https://www.investopedia.com/terms/r/random-variable.asp

23   https://www.investopedia.com/terms/v/virtual-currency.asp

24   https://www.investopedia.com/terms/b/blockchain.asp

25   https://www.investopedia.com/terms/s/simple_interest.asp

26   https://www.investopedia.com/terms/c/compounding.asp

27   https://www.investopedia.com/terms/1/401kplan.asp

28   https://www.investopedia.com/terms/t/tax-advantaged.asp

29   https://www.investopedia.com/terms/1/401kplan.asp

30   https://www.investopedia.com/terms/1/403bplan.asp

31   https://www.federalreserve.gov/aboutthefed/files/the-fed-explained.pdf#page=8

32   https://www.federalreserve.gov/aboutthefed/files/the-fed-explained.pdf#page=14

33   https://www.federalreserve.gov/aboutthefed/files/the-fed-explained.pdf#page=24

34   https://www.federalreserve.gov/aboutthefed/files/the-fed-explained.pdf#page=50

35   https://www.federalreserve.gov/aboutthefed/files/the-fed-explained.pdf#page=66

36 https://www.federalreserve.gov/aboutthefed/files/the-fed-explained.pdf#page=88

37 https://www.federalreserve.gov/aboutthefed/files/the-fed-explained.pdf#page=116

38 https://en.wikipedia.org/wiki/Stocks_for_the_Long_Run#cite_note-1

39 https://en.wikipedia.org/wiki/Stocks_for_the_Long_Run#cite_note-2

40 https://en.wikipedia.org/wiki/Stocks_for_the_Long_Run#cite_note-3

Made in the USA
Middletown, DE
18 September 2022

10117142R00110